KT-197-650

The CONTAINER EXPERT

Dr. D.G.Hessayon

First edition: 150,000 copies

Published 1995
by Expert Books
a division of Transworld Publishers Ltd

Copyright © Dr.D.G.Hessayon 1995

The right of Dr.D.G.Hessayon to be identified
as author of this work has been asserted in accordance
with sections 77 and 78 of the Copyright Designs and
Patents Act 1988.

A catalogue record for this book is available from the British Library

TRANSWORLD PUBLISHERS LTD
61–63 Uxbridge Road, London W5 5SA

 Distributed in the United States
by Sterling Publishing Co., Inc.
387 Park Avenue South,
New York, NY 10016-8810

EXPERT BOOKS

LONDON · NEW YORK · TORONTO · SYDNEY · AUCKLAND

Contents

All rights reserved. No part of this publication may be reproduced, stored in a retrieval system, or transmitted in any form or by any means, electronic, mechanical, photocopying, recording, or otherwise, without the prior permission of the Publishers.

Neither the Publishers nor the Author can accept liability for the use of any of the materials or methods recommended in this book or for any consequences arising out of their use, nor can they be held responsible for any errors or omissions that may be found in the text or may occur at a future date as a result of changes in rules, laws or equipment.

Printed and bound in Great Britain by Jarrold & Sons Ltd, Norwich

ISBN 0 903505 43 6   © D.G.HESSAYON 1995

CHAPTER 1

INTRODUCTION

About 50 years ago nearly all of the bedding plants sold to gardeners each spring were planted out in beds or borders. Today more than half of the bedding plants we buy go into containers rather than the open soil. This fact clearly illustrates that there has been a container revolution in recent years — a dramatic increase in the use of pots, hanging baskets etc around the house and in the garden.

Flower-bedecked tubs and troughs now stand at the fronts and backs of houses down every street, but it is quite wrong to think that container gardening is something new. It is as old as gardening itself — flowering plants were grown in ornate vases in China before the Christian era began, and shrub-filled clay pots were a feature of the gardens in Ancient Greece, Egypt and Rome. Nor is it new in Western Europe — the Grand Gardens of Britain and France have long had their impressive stone urns crammed with flowers or wooden tubs filled with Orange trees. Geranium-filled troughs are a well-established feature of the Swiss and Austrian chalet, and flower-bedecked terracotta pots are part of the landscape of some Mediterranean countries. So we must be careful before assuming that the concept of having a number of containers on the walls and in the garden began with the end of World War II.

But something *has* happened. The concept may have been around for hundreds or even thousands of years but the ordinary gardeners in Britain, America and many other countries did not take it up. For them container-growing was a fringe activity — perhaps a pot or two or a window box and nothing more. Now everything has changed, and it is the fastest-growing sector of the garden scene.

There is no single reason. The spectacular increase in the number of patios has meant that there are bare paved areas to cover and the increase in the number of apartment blocks has meant that there are more balconies to fill. But there is more to it than that. There has been a dramatic growth in the number of different types of container on offer in garden centres, magazines, DIY stores etc. In addition there has been a growing realisation that the garden can be used as an outside room for summer living and that containers provide excellent decoration around the tables and chairs.

Containers everywhere, but it is not easy to agree upon an exact definition. Perhaps the simplest approach is to regard a container as a receptacle for growing plants which is not fully open to the garden soil below. This means that a raised bed created on open ground is a *bed* — when built on paving it is a *container*.

The advantages of growing in a container rather than in a bed or border are set out on page 5, and in addition there is no digging and little or no weeding to do. However, you must never regard it as an 'easy' way to garden. First of all, there are more decisions to make than with open ground gardening. You must choose the right container, and that is not easy with the vast assortment on offer with prices ranging from the very cheap to the ridiculously expensive. Then you must choose a suitable growing medium, the best situation for the container and finally the plants which will flourish in the chosen environment.

In addition to these extra jobs at the planning stage, there is a need for extra care for the growing plants. The amount of soil or compost available to the roots is limited, so the watering and feeding requirements are greater than in the open garden. Frequent watering is essential in summer and this may mean using a watering can or hose daily during a dry spell. Regular feeding every 2–4 weeks may be required. In addition permanent plants in a poorly-insulated pot can suffer in a severe winter — without protection the soil ball may freeze solid.

On the following pages you will learn how to make the right choices and how to satisfy the extra needs described above. But to see how growing in containers can add to the beauty of your home and garden you will have to look around. Look at displays at garden centres, show gardens and other people's houses to see just how varied and attractive plant-filled containers can be.

The Basics

SHAPE

Attractive as an ornament — less so as a container for plants. Area available for planting is small, potting on is difficult and there is an increased risk of winter damage

These standard shapes are generally the best — surface area and volume of growing medium are adequate and soil can readily expand upwards if frozen

The large surface area means that an attractive display can be created, but the lack of depth means that frequent watering will be necessary. Do not plant too close to the edge

SIZE

To avoid very frequent watering the container should be at least 9 in. (22.5 cm) wide and deep. In a container with sloping sides at least 4 in. of compost is essential for even shallow-rooting plants, and a leafy shrub or tree will need a container which is at least 1½ ft (45 cm) wide and 1 ft (30 cm) deep

PLANT

Many types of plants ranging from tall trees to tiny alpines can be grown — see Chapter 3 for details. The planting may be for a permanent display or for a seasonal one which is removed when the flowers have faded

WATERING SPACE

A gap must be left between the top of the container and the surface of the compost or mulch. This space is filled with water at watering time

CONTAINER

The world of containers is dominated by the well-known types such as pots, tubs, window boxes and hanging baskets, but almost any receptacle will do if it has a number of basic properties. It must be waterproof, although clay/terracotta loses water from the surface and hanging baskets need a liner. It must be stable and it must resist rot, rust and corrosion when exposed to the weather — it should also be frost-proof if required for permanent planting. It must be non-toxic to plants and it must hold enough compost to support the plants you intend to grow. Finally, water must drain away quickly. For details of container materials see pages 10–11 — see Chapter 2 for the background to container types

MULCH

An optional extra which is widely used with alpines. A shallow surface layer of crushed stone or gravel reduces water loss and inhibits weed growth

GROWING MEDIUM

Traditionally a soil or peat-based compost is used, but types based on coir etc are now available. The medium must be free-draining and contain a supply of fertilizer. See page 7 for details

DRAINAGE LAYER

In large containers crocking and a layer of gravel are needed — see page 16

DRAINAGE HOLES

Usually but not always present in shop-bought containers. Adequate drainage is vital. Plastic pots often contain numerous small holes. Large terracotta and wooden containers should have at least one hole (½ in. or more across) every 6 in.

LEGS

Bricks, small blocks or shop-bought terracotta legs should be used to raise the container above the ground or paving. This allows free drainage, prevents soil pest entry and reduces the risk of rot in wooden containers

BASE

A firm base is necessary. Exceptions — window boxes, hanging baskets and wall-mounted units

DRIP TRAY
The commonest type is the plastic or terracotta saucer. It acts as a water reservoir, but do not keep it constantly filled with water

or

GROUND or PAVING
Nearly all free-standing containers are stood either on bare earth or a paved area such as a patio. This base must be both firm and level

or

MOVABLE TROLLEY
This is the best type of base if the container is heavy and you intend to move it from one part of the garden to another during the season or indoors in winter

The Advantages of Containers

GROUND IS NOT NEEDED

This is the only way to garden for the millions who live in apartments — containers on the balconies, windows, outside walls and sometimes on the roof take the place of beds and borders. For those with a garden there are still many places for tubs, boxes etc on paved areas, patios, pathways, porches and walls. Plants can be grown right next to the house

BARE OR DULL AREAS CAN BE IMPROVED

The outstanding reason for having planted-up containers in the garden is to add a splash of living colour or shape to an otherwise dull area. Doors and windows can be framed, large expanses of bare wall can be enlivened and the monotony of paved backyards, courtyards, terraces or patios can be removed. An important aspect is the introduction of the third dimension to a purely two-dimensional area

PLANT DISPLAY IS IMPROVED

Flowers, trees and shrubs are given an extra dimension — a bold display can be used as a focal point. Small and fragrant plants are brought closer to eye and nose level and weak-stemmed plants can be allowed to droop and trail. Tender types can be given the protection of a sunny wall

EYESORES CAN BE HIDDEN

Manhole covers can be masked with a collection of movable tubs or pots

PLANTS ARE EASIER TO REACH

This is an important consideration for physically challenged people. Using tall containers can remove the need to stoop for such jobs as planting and dead-heading

PLANTS NOT SUITED TO YOUR SOIL CAN BE GROWN

Your soil may be cold, heavy and badly drained which makes it unsuitable for many plants. With container-growing you can choose a compost which you know will be suitable. By using a lime-free mixture you can have Azaleas, Camellias and so on in a chalky garden and you can grow alpines to perfection on a clayey site

PLANTS CAN BE MOVED ONCE THE DISPLAY IS OVER

A potted Rose bush in full bloom obviously deserves a prime spot in the garden, but once the flowering season is over you can move the container to a less prominent site

PLANTS CAN BE TAKEN WITH YOU WHEN YOU MOVE

Containers and the plants they hold can be taken with you without the need for digging up and then transplanting

LESS CHANCE OF PEST DAMAGE

Plants get a high degree of protection against slugs and some soil pests

TENDER PLANTS CAN BE GROWN OUTDOORS

In the autumn tubs and pots containing tender perennials such as Palms and Orange trees can be brought into a conservatory or greenhouse. The containers are brought out again in the spring when the danger of frost has passed. Small containers can be kept in an unheated room if you do not have a greenhouse

TRAILING PLANTS CAN BE PROPERLY DISPLAYED

Many annual and perennial flowers and foliage plants have a pendent growth habit — Basket Begonias, Black-eyed Susan and so on. These cannot be used as trailers in the open garden but in a container their cascading stems can be properly displayed

The Places for Containers

FRONT DOOR & PORCH

This is an excellent site for containers, either singly or as a pair of matched tubs or pots. For a formal look you can add a touch of elegance by having a half-barrel with a topiary-trimmed tree on either side of the door. For a more informal look you can have containers filled with bright upright and trailing flowers which are changed with the seasons. Whichever approach you adopt it will be essential to select and maintain both the containers and plants with care. No other garden feature will be as closely inspected by your visitors, so the display must always be in first-class condition

BALCONY & ROOFTOP

The balcony is a prime site in several European countries. A line of window boxes are placed on the paving at the base of the railings or are attached to their tops or front. The boxes are then filled with an assortment of bright flowers or a single species of a pendent plant and the stems trail down the wall below the balcony. For floor-standing displays you should use a lightweight container and a peat-based compost. Exposure to strong winds and the need for regular watering can be a problem. The rooftop garden is an enlarged version of the decorated balcony but is not designed to improve the external appearance of the house

FOCAL POINT

A large and impressive container or a group of smaller containers can be used to provide a focal point in the garden. Attractive trees and shrubs have an important role to play here. Both the pot and the plants it contains must be in scale with the surroundings

WALL

Hanging baskets are a popular feature these days — about a third of gardens have at least one. The best site for a basket or wall pot is partly sunny during the day and protected from strong winds. Remember that daily watering may be needed in summer

PATIO

This is the favourite place these days for free-standing containers. The starkness of bare walls and paving slabs is relieved by the presence of plants. Think carefully about siting. Grouping pots and tubs together is usually more effective than dotting them about the patio. Avoid the main pedestrian routes and consider a climbing plant or two against the house wall. Also consider shrubs, trees and fruit — you don't have to stick to the usual bedding plants and bulbs

WINDOW SILL

Window boxes add colour and interest to the front of houses, apartment blocks, offices and public buildings. Temporary plants are generally used for a spring/summer display, but part or all of the planting can be permanent. Read the section on window boxes before buying, fixing and filling one. The construction material and colour should not detract from the plants and ease of window opening should not be hampered. Make sure it is firmly attached

PATH & STEPS

A line of identical pots or troughs can enhance the appearance of a plain path, driveway or flight of steps. A word of warning — on no account should the containers or the plants hinder free movement. If the path or steps are narrow then the containers should be placed at one or either end of the path or stairs

POND

There are two basic uses here. Water Lilies and many other aquatic plants are planted in submerged baskets within the pond — outside the pond more conventional containers are used close to the edge to provide floral interest. A minipond for a Water Lily and an aquatic plant or two can be made in a half-barrel or large trough

The Growing Medium

It is vitally important to choose a satisfactory growing medium for your container. This relatively small amount of material has to support the roots, provide enough water to ensure vigorous growth and yet be free-draining enough to prevent waterlogging. It must contain enough fertilizer to give the new plants a good start in life and it must have the right acidity or alkalinity for the types you have chosen.

Ordinary soil taken straight from the garden is not suitable. The major problem is that regular watering plus its restriction in a pot or trough are almost bound to lead to a complete loss of structure. The answer is to use either a planting mixture or a compost. The right choice will depend upon the size of the container and the type of plant.

For growing trees and vigorous shrubs in large containers or raised beds

▼

PLANTING MIXTURE

For growing every sort of plant in nearly all container types

▼

COMPOST

• PLANTING MIXTURE •

Planting mixture is a growing medium which is based on unsterilised soil. It is made at home using loam — a soil which is neither heavy and sticky nor light and gritty. Use garden soil if it is suitable or buy some if your ground is poor — make sure that no roots of perennial weeds are present. Moisten the ingredients before blending.

4 parts Loam

2 parts Peat

1 part Sharp Sand

Slow-release fertilizer — according to maker's instructions

Chalk (5 gm per bucketful) — omit for lime-hating plants

• COMPOST •

Compost is a growing medium which is based on sterilised soil or a bulky organic material such as peat, coir or treated manure. For the vast majority of containers it is better to choose a shop-bought compost rather than a home-made planting mixture. A wide and puzzling array will be found at any DIY store or garden centre, so it is necessary to know a few rules. The first one is to buy fresh material — avoid bags which have faded print or are badly stained. The second rule is to consider the advantages and disadvantages of the various types before making your choice.

Soil-based Compost

The base here is good quality topsoil which has been sterilised to get rid of weeds, pests and disease organisms. Peat is added and the mixture is blended with sharp sand, lime and fertilizer. There are two important advantages compared with soilless composts. The first one is extra weight — this means extra stability for the container and enhanced support for large plants. The second advantage is its ability to hold nutrients so that less regular feeding is required. It is the preferred choice for permanent planting in free-standing containers. Several grades are available:

John Innes No.2 — for most seasonal planting
John Innes No.3 — for permanent planting and vigorous seasonal planting
Ericaceous (no lime added) — for lime-hating plants

Soilless Compost

Because loam is difficult to obtain and its quality is variable, most modern composts are soilless ones and are usually based on peat or peat and sand. They have several advantages over soil-based ones. Their quality does not vary and they are lighter and cleaner to handle. Disadvantages include the difficulty of re-wetting if the compost is allowed to dry out, and feeding must begin after a couple of months. It is the preferred choice where weight would be a problem (window boxes, hanging baskets etc) and for short-term planting. Several grades are available:

Peat-based — well-known and reliable, but some people do not like to use peat
Coir-based — the usual peat substitute. Some experts praise it but others do not
Ericaceous (no lime added) — for lime-hating plants

OPTIONAL EXTRAS

Water-holding granules

Polymer crystals which hold up to 400 times their own weight of water. Claimed to cut down watering needs — not all experts agree

Slow-release fertilizers

Tablets, cones and sticks of controlled-release plant food are available which are inserted in the compost and then feed for months

CHAPTER 2
TYPES OF CONTAINERS

One of the treats of visiting a garden centre or the gardening section of a superstore is to look at the ever-expanding range of containers on offer. Unfortunately, most are bought by getting the right answers to two questions — 'Can I afford it?' and 'Do I like it?'.

Both questions are of course important but do be careful of the answers. Firstly the question of price. A really inexpensive plastic tub or trough might be quite suitable if you intend to cover the face with trailing plants and if you don't expect it to last for many years, but it would be quite unsuitable as an item to serve as a focal point or an attractive feature when bare in winter. The question of personal likes and dislikes is important, but finding it attractive does not necessarily make it a good buy.

The point is that you should ask a lot more than two questions, and you should begin your questioning in the garden and not in the shop, magazine advertising columns or garden show stand. The prime question is — Where will the container go? The purpose of a container or group of containers is to add living greenery, shape and colour to an area which requires visual improvement — see page 6 for suggested sites. Having chosen the spot, the next question concerns size. Should the hanging basket be a small or large one? How wide and deep is the sill for the window box? Should the container be tall or squat? To some extent the right answers to this question are governed by the types of plant you wish to grow. It is obvious that a tree or shrub will have to have a much larger container than would be necessary for bedding plants and bulbs.

Now you have some idea of place, size and plant types it is time to think about practical considerations. The first one concerns watering. However much you like the idea of hanging baskets and window boxes it is necessary to remember that watering can be a chore. If you know you will not have the time to water regularly or if the container will be placed in an awkward spot, then look for a window box which is as deep and high as possible and a hanging basket which is self-watering.

Next comes weight. A heavy container will be blessed with stability in the garden or patio, but may not be suitable for a balcony or roof garden. The final step at home is to look through all the drawings and photographs in this chapter. The range is by no means exhaustive but you may well be surprised by the number of types available.

You should now be able to pick a suitable container from your garden centre, hardware store, mail order catalogue or magazine, provided you have a clear picture of the colours and textures of the area you have chosen. Take along a photograph if mental pictures are difficult.

If the range in the shop or catalogue is large then some of the containers on offer should meet the requirements you noted at home. Now you must ask 'Is it right for the situation and is it right for me?' As a general rule you should always choose a material, surface and style which will be in keeping with the proposed environment. Older houses, cottage gardens etc call for wood, reconstituted stone and terracotta whereas the simple lines of concrete, terracotta and good quality plastic may fit in well with the clean-cut lines of a modern home. Do not follow this rule *too* slavishly — a contrast sometimes works very well! Be careful with the question of personal appeal. You are not buying an ornament — you are buying a container which should be attractive when the plants are absent or dormant but should not be so showy that it detracts from the plant display. Think twice before choosing shiny plastic or bright colours.

So far we have dealt only with the shop-bought container, but as clearly outlined in this chapter there is an important place for both the home-made container and the 'converted' type — a suitable receptacle which was not constructed as a container but can be turned into one. Shop-bought, home-made or converted, the container should be soundly constructed and with the exception of hanging baskets should be filled after being stood in or attached to its new home, not carried to it with its load of compost. And now it's planting time, but for that you will have to wait for Chapter 3.

Main Types

FREE-STANDING MULTIPURPOSE
pages 12–19

The basic type of container found on the patio, pathway, porch etc. Included here are the standard pot, tub, trough and urn. It does not require support and is not designed for any particular type of plant

FREE-STANDING SPECIFIC
pages 20–21

A special type of pot, barrel or basket made of wood, plastic or terracotta. It does not require support and is designed for a particular type of plant or plant group, such as Potatoes, Strawberries, small bulbs, herbs or aquatics

WINDOW BOX
pages 22–25

A trough for attachment above or below the sill. Many types are available in plastic, fibreglass, metal and terracotta, but wood is the preferred material. Permanent planting is possible but seasonal displays are more popular

HANGING BASKET
pages 26–31

A container which is suspended from a hook or bracket and supports a plant display which is rounded, hemispherical or globular. The traditional type is made from wire, but solid-wall and self-watering ones are now popular

WALL MOUNTED
pages 32–33

A bowl or trough which is related to the hanging basket, but is attached to a wall rather than being suspended. Many types are available in terracotta, plastic, reconstituted stone, wood, wire and wrought iron

TOWER
page 34

A novel type of container which is becoming increasingly popular. Materials, sizes and shapes differ widely and it may be free-standing or supported, but all share the property of producing a display which is clearly column-like

GROWING BAG
page 35

A ready-filled container more often used under glass than in the open garden. The compost within the thin plastic pillow is used for vegetables, soft fruit or bedding plants. Inexpensive, but of no decorative value

CONVERTED
pages 36–37

A 'converted' container is any receptacle which is used for growing plants outdoors but which was not initially designed for that purpose. Examples include sinks, chimney pots, wheelbarrows and plastic buckets

RAISED BED
page 38

A permanent container made with bricks, stone, reconstituted stone blocks or railway sleepers and filled with a soil-based planting mixture. The units can be laid by the dry-wall method or be bonded with mortar

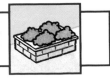

POT HOLDER
page 39

A receptacle made of metal, plastic or terracotta which may look like a container but is actually designed to hold one or more planted-up containers. These containers may or may not be hidden by the pot holder

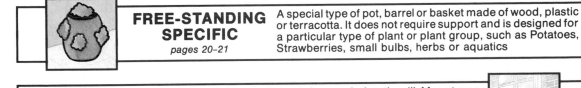

Materials

WOOD

CLAY/ TERRACOTTA

Baked clay is probably the oldest of all container materials, and for many gardeners it has no equal. The colour is attractive and it develops a patina with age. It also breathes, which means that the compost is less likely to overheat in summer or become water-logged in winter than the growing medium in a waterproof container. Many beautiful types are available, but it is hard to generalise about price. The cheap and humble clay plant pot is machine made with its practical purpose rather than beauty in mind. Terracotta is refined clay in which additives may be incorporated. The cheaper sorts may be machine made, but the expensive and highly ornate types are made on a potter's wheel or moulded by hand. There are three problems. All baked clay containers are brittle and will break if dropped, and their porous nature means that they need more frequent watering than plastic ones. The final drawback is the danger of frost damage, and price is no indication of frost resistance. For permanent planting on an exposed site choose terracotta containers with a frost-proof guarantee.

Wood is extremely practical and is suitable for most situations — thick wood is an excellent heat-insulator. Whether the container is shop-bought or do-it-yourself, make sure that there are no hidden problems. Most containers are made from one of the softwoods, so the timber must be treated with a non-toxic preservative. If you buy a rot-proof hardwood container then ensure that there is a label stating that the wood has come from a managed forest. Look for rust-proof screws and avoid nails. The most popular timber container is the half-barrel — make sure that all the staves are sound and close-fitting, and the metal bands should be secure. Do not let the wood of the barrel dry out when not in use.

METAL

In the old days free-standing containers were frequently made of lead, iron and bronze, but not any more. The price is prohibitive for most gardeners and antique ones have become collectors' items. Metal household objects of copper, brass etc are occasionally used as 'converted' containers — see page 36. The inside should be treated with a bitumen paint before use. White-coated aluminium is sometimes used for ornate pot holders (page 39), but the only widespread use of metal these days is as coated or treated wire for the manufacture of hanging baskets, wall-mounted containers etc.

PLASTIC

It is not surprising that plastic containers are so popular. They are lightweight, durable, usually inexpensive and available in a wide range of finishes, colours, sizes and shapes. The basic point is that you get what you pay for. At the garden centre you will find numerous examples of thin-walled plastic containers in white, black, green and brown and a glossy surface. Polythene is the usual material — the price is low but so are heat insulation and permanence. At the other end of the scale you should be able to buy a stout container made from a heavy-duty plastic such as polypropylene, polystyrene and polyurethane. These do not fade and crack after a few years in the same way as cheap plastic, and some have good insulation properties.

FIBRE

This material is easy to recognise — it looks like brown papier-mâché and is generally made from recycled paper. Fibre (sometimes referred to as a resin-bonded cellulose fibre) is used for bowls and troughs — these containers have little decorative value but the surface can be hidden by means of trailing plants. Lack of permanence is the problem — they last for only 2-3 years, but there are advantages. The fibre trough is light, cheap and biodegradable.

STONE

Real stone with a scattering of moss and lichens is perhaps the most admired of the traditional materials. In the right setting it is very effective, but for most people and situations it is too heavy and too expensive. The urn in a type of stone ranging from gritty sandstone to polished marble is the usual form — ornate carving of the surface is attractive, but rather pointless if you plan to grow trailing plants. Make sure that drainage is adequate and do not plant acid-loving types in limestone. These days old stone sinks and farm troughs are eagerly sought for use as alpine gardens (see page 68).

CONCRETE

Concrete is the least expensive but also the least attractive of the 'stone' materials. An exposed-aggregate surface helps to improve the appearance, but fine moulding is not possible. Still, concrete does have its place. Large containers in simple shapes can look quite at home in a modern setting, and the thick wall ensures good insulation in winter. Always allow a new concrete container to weather before filling with compost and planting. Glass-reinforced cement looks more like reconstituted stone than concrete. It is used to manufacture modern-style containers in simple shapes.

RECONSTITUTED STONE

These are the 'stone' containers you will see everywhere. They have much of the look of real stone but are considerably cheaper and are available in a much wider range of shapes and sizes. Their popularity continues to increase but reconstituted stone is not new — this material was used for containers in the 18th century. The concrete/crushed stone mix is cast as urns, troughs, pots, blocks, tubs etc. The surface may look stark when new — to age it and promote lichen formation you should paint the container with a yoghurt/liquid manure mixture. If on the other hand you want to keep the surface clean then water and a cloth should be used — never a stiff or wire brush. Reconstituted stone blocks are widely used for raised bed construction — see page 38.

FIBREGLASS

Fibreglass is an excellent and versatile material with several virtues. It is much less expensive than real stone and it is much lighter than reconstituted stone. It is durable, easy to transport and is moulded into tubs, window boxes, planters etc. Plain and smooth-surfaced types are available, but you can also find ones patterned and coloured to look like stone, wood, lead etc. As with all materials there are drawbacks. Fibreglass is somewhat brittle and may chip or crack if dropped. Its insulation capacity is poor, so the compost may freeze in winter and overheat in summer. Stability can be a problem if a soilless compost is used — add a base of gravel if the site is exposed and the container is tall and narrow.

TUFA

A truly surprising material. Tufa is a form of magnesium limestone which is porous and can hold more than its own weight of water — in addition plant roots will grow in it. A piece can be planted up with alpines and stood on a patio or balcony — the rock is soft and can be worked quite easily with a drill or chisel. Make a series of downward sloping holes 1 in. (2.5 cm) wide and 4 in. (10 cm) deep. Insert small rockery plants and plug in with a gritty compost. Keep the rock moist in dry weather.

GLAZED EARTHENWARE

You will find them in most garden centres — pots with an unglazed creamy white interior and a shiny glazed exterior in various colours. These Oriental pots are not for every garden, but in the right situation can be extremely effective. They are best planted with a single specimen shrub or tree with strong architectural lines — Palm, Japanese Maple, Phormium etc. Remember that strong patterning or bold lettering on the surface can detract from the plant display.

CONTAINER TYPE:
FREE-STANDING MULTIPURPOSE

Grouped here are the containers which are so often seen nowadays on patios, terraces, walkways and so on. These are the ones which can be used for all sorts of bedding plants, trees, shrubs, bulbs etc — the containers designed for specific plants such as Strawberries, Potatoes and Water Lilies are dealt with on pages 20–21.

The shapes and sizes of these multipurpose free-standing containers vary greatly and so do the materials used in their construction. A variety of names are used to describe these various types — pots, troughs, vases, jars etc, but unfortunately there are no generally agreed definitions for them. The planter shown in one catalogue may be listed as a pot or tub in another.

Set out below is a simple classification which serves as a glossary for the various containers described or illustrated in this book — a useful guide, but the dividing line between the various types is often blurred.

As noted on page 4 it is important to make sure that there are adequate drainage holes at the base, but a few of the examples shown on the following pages do have self-watering versions. Here the base is fitted with some form of water reservoir.

POT
(Other types included: **Jar**, **Vase**)
Compost surface area*
small or moderate

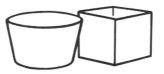

TUB
(Other types included: **Box, Planter**)
Compost surface area*
large

BOWL
(Other types included: **Shallow Planter, Tray**)
Compost surface area*
very large

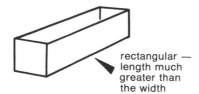

rectangular — length much greater than the width

TROUGH
Compost surface area*
moderate or large

handles may be present

pedestal

URN
Compost surface area*
small, moderate or large

strip metal frame with inner liner

BASKET
Compost surface area*
very large

* **Compost surface area** is the extent of the compost at the top compared to the height of the container

Pots

STANDARD PLANT POT

This is the most popular free-standing container, available in many sizes and several different materials. The basic shape is square or round with gently sloping sides and the basic materials are ordinary clay, high quality terracotta and inexpensive plastic. It is generally employed where the plant and not the container is the decorative feature and where the amount of plant material is not extensive. It may be rimmed or rimless, glazed or unglazed and with or without a saucer. Choose a **half pot** where a larger compost surface area is required

LONG TOM POT

An old-fashioned type for the back of a group of pots. Useful for trailing plants, but stability can be a problem — not often seen at garden centres

GARLAND POT

This type of pot has a decorative surface. The garland of leaves, fruits etc may be simple or complex. Sometimes called a **swag pot**

CYLINDRICAL POT

Available in terracotta, plastic and reconstituted stone. Surface may be moulded — e.g a **cherub pot**. Sometimes called a **chimney pot**

ORANGE POT

A wide-mouthed pot with a prominent ridge around the body. Once used for displaying Orange trees. Other name — **Roman vase**

BELL POT

An attractive shape — an upturned bell with a flat base. Both unglazed terracotta and glazed earthenware are widely available

ORIENTAL POT

Many types available — the glazed surface may be muted or colourful and lettering or plant motifs may be an added feature

STANDARD JAR

This differs from a pot by having a restricted neck. Less suitable than a pot for growing plants, but a jar can be a focal point feature, especially where a Mediterranean or Oriental effect is sought

ALI BABA JAR

A popular terracotta jar — the basic features are a strong rim at the top and the widest part is just below the neck. Usually large

CRETAN JAR

The widest part is the centre of the jar — handles may be present. Known as a **beehive jar** when the surface has a series of ridges

WINE JAR

A jar with a narrow base and large handles is often referred to as a wine jar. Here the container itself is the main decorative feature

MULTIPOT

Several terracotta pots fused together — a number of brands are available. Not for the purist, perhaps, but can be eye-catching

VASE

An unusual shape — a flower-vase shaped pot in terracotta with an extended base for stability. Not very practical

Tubs

HALF-BARREL

Wooden half-barrels are now specially made for use as plant containers. Plastic, reconstituted stone and fibreglass versions are also available

VERSAILLES TUB

The traditional container for Orange trees and topiary. Stained or painted wood is the standard material, but plastic and fibreglass ones can be bought

GERANIUM POT

A wide-mouthed container which is a tub rather than a pot. The distinctive feature is a series of narrow ridges around the terracotta surface. Good, but no longer popular

MODERN PLANTER

Clean, uncluttered and without ornament — a good choice in the right situation. The usual materials are plastic, concrete, fibreglass and reconstituted stone

TRADITIONAL PLANTER

The surface is textured or ornamented. Basic shapes are round, oval or square and the materials are stone, metal, terracotta, plastic and reconstituted stone

QUADRANT PLANTER

A triangular container which can be used in various ways. The usual situation is in a corner, but four can be fitted together to form a large square for planting herbs etc

Bowls

ROUND BOWL

Modern-style versions are made from fibreglass, plastic or concrete. Ornamented traditional ones such as the **Romanesque bowl** are moulded in reconstituted stone

ROUND CONE

An eye-catching shape, but drying out of plants near the edge can be a problem. Metal supports are used to hold cones with a pointed base. For seasonal planting only

HALF-BARREL

An unusual version of the standard half-barrel shown above — in this 'bowl' version the compost surface area is increased for bedding plants or bulbs

GOTHIC BOWL

Hexagonal and octagonal bowls are available — they can be stood singly or fitted together to form a complex pattern. The Gothic version is ornamented as above

ORIENTAL BOWL

Shallow versions of the Oriental pot shown on page 13 are available in a variety of colours, including the attractive blue (Ishing) glaze. Useful in an Oriental pot group

Troughs

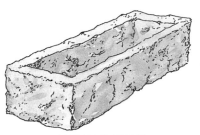

STONE TROUGH

Stone troughs are hard to find these days, but excellent reconstituted stone ones can be bought. Use for rock garden plants — see page 68. An artificial stone trough can be made from a sink — see page 36

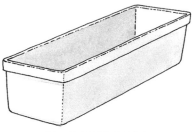

PLASTIC TROUGH

Shiny plastic troughs are widely available from garden centres and DIY stores. They are inexpensive and lightweight, but there are no other virtues. Cover surface with trailers to improve appearance

WOODEN TROUGH

A good choice, combining a natural appearance with a reasonable price. Many types are available including DIY ones, rustic faced troughs, hardwood and softwood, stained and painted

DECORATED TROUGH

Carved stone troughs are a feature of the grand garden, but are extremely expensive nowadays. An acceptable alternative is one of the reconstituted stone or fibreglass ones. Many patterns are on offer

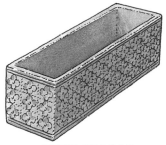

METAL TROUGH

Antique lead, iron and copper containers are very expensive. You can find modern ones in traditional patterns which have been cast from lead, faux (false) lead and bronzage (bronze-resin compound)

Urns

SHALLOW URN

A shallow urn in the right setting can make a good focal point, but it is not a top-quality container for plants. The limited amount of compost means that the range of suitable plants is restricted and frequent watering will be necessary in summer

DEEP URN

A plastic urn filled with bedding plants may be suitable for the patio but will not do as a key feature in a prime spot. Choose reconstituted stone or top-quality fibreglass with a stone or lead finish. The urn surface may be plain or ornate — make sure it fits in with garden style

Baskets

METAL BASKET

Free-standing baskets are now available at garden centres or by mail order. A water-retaining liner is placed at the base of the strip metal container and after planting a hanging basket effect is created. Illustrated above is the Babyllon Bowl

Filling the Container

STEP 1:
PREPARE THE CONTAINER
A new container should require little or no preparation. New and raw softwood must be treated with a water-based preservative — the inside of a half-barrel can be charred with a blowlamp for protection against rot. The outside of wooden containers can be coated with an exterior-grade varnish or paint. Bore drainage holes in the tub, pot, trough etc if they are absent. Drill plastic, fibreglass, earthenware and terracotta slowly at low speed to prevent cracking or splintering — cover the top and bottom surfaces with adhesive tape before you begin to drill. Previously used containers should be cleaned thoroughly before filling. Scrub if necessary. Check the inside of a wooden container for rot. All new or used porous receptacles should be soaked overnight before Step 2

STEP 6:
PLANT UP THE CONTAINER
As mentioned elsewhere in this book you should buy top-quality planting material and set the plants more closely together than you would do in the open garden. Follow the steps described on page 17. A 1–2 in. (2.5–5 cm) deep watering space should be present after planting. Water in immediately even if rain is forecast

STEP 4:
ADD THE PEAT LAYER
A peat layer is not necessary if the container is reasonably small. If the unit is large then you can use peat to reduce the amount of compost you will need — the compost layer need be no more than 9 in. (22.5 cm) deep

STEP 5:
ADD THE COMPOST LAYER
Use one of the compost or planting mixtures described on page 7. It should be moist but not wet and should be poured or shovelled into the container until it is almost full. Press this compost layer down gently with your hands. If the unit is large then add the compost as a series of layers, pressing down each one before adding the next layer

STEP 3:
ADD THE DRAINAGE LAYER
A drainage layer is not necessary if the container has a number of small holes and a soilless compost is to be used. Where this does not apply the drainage hole or holes should be covered by crocks (pieces of broken plastic or clay pots) as shown or by pieces of fine mesh screen. If the unit is a large one add a layer of rubble or gravel to help drainage and stability — omit this stone layer if weight is a problem

STEP 2:
PUT THE CONTAINER IN PLACE
Whenever possible set the container in place at the chosen site before going on to Step 3 — dragging a heavy unit complete with compost and plants along the ground or paving can lead to breakage or damage. Even the empty container may be far too heavy to lift if it is made of concrete or reconstituted stone. The method of transport here depends on shape and size. If the unit is fairly shallow and wide it can be placed on a large polythene bag or sheet and the plastic then pulled along the ground to the site. If the container is too tall or too heavy for this method you will either have to lever it carefully into a wheelbarrow or use a sack trolley. Once at the chosen location the container should be stood on blocks or short legs to raise the drainage holes above the surface

Planting & Potting

A receptacle becomes a *container* when plants are put into it. Without plants the decorative receptacle in the garden is an *ornament*. Plants are set into a container by either planting or potting, and these two terms do not mean the same thing. **Planting** involves setting the rootball in a hole which has been dug or scooped out of the compost. **Potting** involves setting the rootball on a layer of compost and then filling in around it with more compost.

PLANTING

Plan the design first if several plants are to be put into the container. Water the pots thoroughly and allow to drain before you begin. Make sure that the growing medium in the container is moist. Plants raised under glass should have been properly hardened off.

① Start with the largest plant. Dig a hole in the compost. Make sure that the hole is large enough for the rootball by inserting the pot into it — remove more compost if the pot does not fit easily

② Remove the plant from the pot as shown below. With container-grown plants cut down the side and remove cover carefully. Put the rootball in the hole — the top of the rootball should be at or just below the surface

③ Firm in by replacing some of the compost removed by the trowel and then pressing down with your fingers. Continue planting — finish off with the edging plants. Smooth the compost

④ Planting is now finished — note that any staking which is required should have been done before the plants were set in the holes. With permanent planting cover the top with chippings or bark. Water in gently

POTTING

POTTING ON

This is carried out when a single large plant is to be put into a container or the roots have filled the pot and the plant is starting to become pot-bound. Tell-tale signs are roots growing through the drainage hole, compost which dries out very quickly, and slow growth despite favourable conditions. If the plant is pot-bound it is generally necessary to pot on.

① A suitable sequence of pot sizes is an increase of 2–3 in. (5–7.5 cm) in diameter at each potting on stage. Stop when the desired plant size is reached. Scrub out old pots thoroughly — soak clay ones overnight

② Water the plant. One hour later remove it from the pot as shown above. If difficult to dislodge, knock the pot on the edge of a hard surface and run a knife around the rootball. Remove old crocks

③ Cover drainage hole of a clay pot with crocks. Add a layer of potting compost. Place the plant on top of this layer — gradually fill surrounding space with damp potting compost. Firm down with your thumbs

④ Tap the pot several times on a hard surface — leave a 1 in. (2.5 cm) watering space. Water thoroughly using a fine rose. In hot and dry weather keep the pot in a shady spot if possible for about a week

REPOTTING

This technique is carried out when the plant is pot-bound and it/or the container has reached the desired or maximum size. During the dormant season remove the plant as above and tease some of the old compost away from the rootball — a small handfork is the usual tool for this work. Trim away some of the root tips, but do not reduce the rootball size by more than 25 per cent. Pot up as described above, using the same size of pot.

The ornate pot and plain trough of reconstituted stone show the versatility of this material. These containers would fit in to most settings, but not a rustic or cottage one ▷

◁ *Shallow bowls are difficult to manage because they need frequent watering, but they do have their place. This one with overhanging flowers covers an unsightly manhole cover*

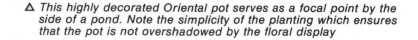

△ *This highly decorated Oriental pot serves as a focal point by the side of a pond. Note the simplicity of the planting which ensures that the pot is not overshadowed by the floral display*

A lattice-sided wooden Versailles tub ▷ — unstained and unpainted with a grass-green inner liner. The muted colours give an extra brilliance to the spring display of Wallflowers and Pansies

◁ The simple plant pot — terracotta on the left and plastic on the right. No ornamentation, no eye-catching shape, but still the most popular free-standing container in the garden

△ Clever planting in a white-painted iron urn. The blues of the Lobelias and the pinks of the Geraniums bring into sharp contrast the creams and yellows of the climbing Roses against the wall

CONTAINER TYPE:
FREE-STANDING SPECIFIC

A number of container types have names which describe a specific use — strawberry barrel, herb pot, bonsai bowl etc. The plant type named is obviously the traditional use for the container, but in some cases it is not the only one which can be grown. Alpines are sometimes planted in herb pots, herbs are grown in strawberry barrels and so on.

BONSAI BOWL

Bonsai trees are sometimes grown in deep pots but the usual container is a shallow bowl. The bonsai bowl may be round, oval, square or oblong and is made of terracotta or earthenware. The surface is generally glazed and various colours are available

STRAWBERRY BARREL

Once the only type was a wooden barrel in which holes had been bored, as shown above. Treat all exposed surfaces with a preservative. Nowadays plastic barrels are available in kit and ready-to-use form. See page 89 for recommended varieties

STRAWBERRY POT

A terracotta or plastic jar for growing Strawberries, small bulbs, herbs or alpines. Watering can be a problem — add grit to the compost and keep moist but not saturated

HERB POT

Smaller than a strawberry pot with fewer but larger and more prominently lipped holes for planting a variety of herbs. Water carefully — follow strawberry pot advice

CROCUS POT

The holes in the sides of this terracotta pot do not have a lip — small bulbs (Crocus, Sparaxis, Scilla, Muscari etc) are pushed into the compost. Avoid waterlogging

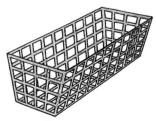

PARSLEY POT

Yet another variation on the pierced pot theme. In this case the container is tower-like and the non-lipped holes are small. Seeds of Parsley or other herbs are pushed through the holes into the moist compost

POTATO BARREL

A round plastic barrel in kit or ready-to-use form. The potato barrel is a purely practical container to enable people without a garden to grow Potatoes. See page 85 for planting instructions

AQUATIC BASKET

It is better to plant aquatics in perforated plastic containers (large size: **Water Lily basket**) than in soil at the bottom of the pond. The basket is lined with hessian before use — louvred baskets do not need lining

A crocus pot with plants in full ▷
flower. This domed-shaped
arrangement illustrates how a
display of small spring bulbs can
be enhanced by growing them in
this type of container

◁ There is no reason why you should not
grow Parsley in an ordinary plant pot, but
this method produces an attractive ferny-
leaved column as well as an abundant
supply of the herb

△ Strawberry and herb pots can be used for flowers as well
as for food crops. In this lipped container a group of
Universal Pansies provides colour from autumn until spring

CONTAINER TYPE:
WINDOW BOX

For the millions who live in apartments the window box is often the only involvement with outdoor gardening. The garden owner has much wider scope for his or her activity, but window boxes do have a special place in exterior home decoration for every-one. They add colour and interest to dull walls and windows, and are an important part of container gardening, but there are a number of rules to follow in order to ensure success and safety.

The construction material and its colour should be chosen with care. It is vital to make sure that they are in keeping with the style of the house, and they should not detract from the plant display. You can buy plastic, metal, terracotta or concrete ones but the preferred material is wood which is either painted or stained. Both surface treatments are satisfactory, but softwood must be protected with some form of plant-safe wood preservative.

Size is also important. A minimum depth and width of 8 in. (20 cm) is required — less than this and your plants will dry out too quickly. Ideally the length of the box should be just a couple of inches less than the sill length. Secure fixing is essential, especially with boxes attached to upstairs windows, and frequent watering is vital. Positioning is important — sunny windows are perhaps the most satisfactory but with shade-loving plants such as Begonia and Impatiens you can create eye-catching displays against a north-facing wall. Watering is a problem — window boxes receive less rain than a container in the open and the amount of compost is strictly limited. Don't use window boxes in a location where watering will be a death-defying feat. Always attach the empty box to the wall before filling and planting — moving a filled box can be dangerous.

There is no reason why you cannot make your own box out of wood, and this is sometimes necessary if your windows are an odd size. Buy ¾ in. (2 cm) thick hardwood boards or preservative-treated softwood. Use water-resistant glue and brass screws. Drill ½–¾ in. (2 cm) drainage holes in the base at 4–6 in. (10–15 cm) intervals.

Fixing

The preferred method of attachment will depend on the type of sill and window. You must choose one of the techniques illustrated below.

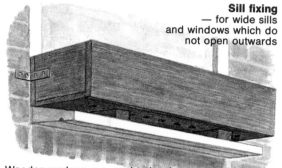

Sill fixing
— for wide sills and windows which do not open outwards

Wooden wedges are used to level the box on the sloping sill and to allow water to drain away. Angle brackets secure the box to the wall

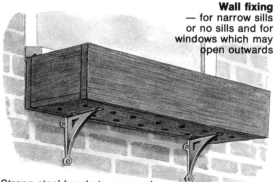

Wall fixing
— for narrow sills or no sills and for windows which may open outwards

Strong steel brackets are used to support the box — make sure screws and wall fixings are large enough for the weight to be carried. Also screw the back of the box to the wall

Types

UNLINED WINDOW BOX

The standard type — compost is placed directly into the window box. Attaching these containers takes time and trouble, so buy the best ones you can afford

LINED WINDOW BOX

One or more liners to hold the compost are included — a useful feature if you want the box to look in tip-top condition at all times. See the Planting section on page 23

SELF-WATERING WINDOW BOX

Some models have a built-in water reservoir — well worth the extra money if daily watering in a hot dry summer is not practical. Plastic and fibreglass are the usual materials

Filling

STEP 4:
PLANT UP THE CONTAINER

Plant firmly — follow the instructions on page 17. Put bedding plants or bulbs closer together than you would in the open garden. A 1 in. (2.5 cm) watering space should be present after planting. This is not the only method of planting up a window box — see below

STEP 1:
ATTACH THE BOX TO THE WALL

Secure the empty box to the wall before filling and planting — moving a filled box can be dangerous. Use strong steel brackets — make sure fixings are large enough to support the weight to be carried. An optional extra for some models is a drip tray filled with gravel below the drainage holes. This will prevent water dripping down the walls

STEP 3:
ADD THE COMPOST LAYER

Add moist soilless compost and gently press each layer down with your hands

STEP 2:
ADD THE DRAINAGE LAYER

Cover the drainage holes with crocks or a fine mesh screen. Add a 1 in. (2.5 cm) layer of gravel to help drainage — omit this layer if weight is a problem

STEP 5:
FOLLOW THE AFTERCARE RULES

As with all containers the compost within must not be allowed to dry out. Gently fill the watering space above the compost with water if the surface is dry. Watering every day may be necessary if the weather is hot and dry during the summer months. Watering upstairs window boxes may be difficult. A number of gadgets including extension lances are available — see Chapter 5. Start to feed with a liquid fertilizer 8 weeks after planting. Use a high potash fertilizer — repeat as recommended on the pack

Planting

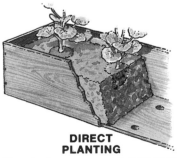

DIRECT PLANTING

The plants are removed from pots, strips, trays etc and put directly into the compost-filled box. The most popular way of planting up, but not necessarily the best as the newly planted specimens are on display while they are becoming established in their new home

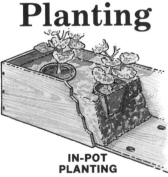

IN-POT PLANTING

The plants are retained in their pots — the window box is filled with peat or gravel. The advantages here are that there is no check to the plants after setting out and pots can be simply taken out and replaced once peak flowering is over. Rampant growers are kept in check

LINER PLANTING

A useful technique which should be more widely practised. The thin plastic or polythene sheet and wire mesh liner is filled with compost and then planted up. Once established it is set in the window box to replace the liner containing plants which have passed their display period

Plants

The height of upright plants is, of course, a key factor. If the specimens are too small then one may be denied seeing them from inside the house, but if they are too large the light entering the room may be seriously reduced. This means that not all the plants in the various lists in Chapter 3 can be used, but this is made up for by the fact that a number of delicate outdoor plants and a number of house plants can flourish in the shelter of a south-facing window.

The choice is up to you and there are no hard-and-fast rules. Trailing plants tumbling over the edge are nearly always an attractive feature and large gaps between plants are usually unattractive. The most popular planting pattern is a display of bulbs and spring-flowering bedding plants at the start of the year and a mixed assembly of popular bedding plants in summer. Many garden designers feel that this is not the best planting pattern. Window boxes cannot be taken down like a hanging basket when the display is over, so it is a good idea to have a year-round green skeleton which is seasonally enlivened with bedding plants.

Climbers at the sides to clamber up trelliswork can be an eye-catching feature. Some plants (Nasturtium, Thunbergia, Ivy etc) can be used as climbers or trailers. Bulbs are widely used to enhance the spring display — use compact types such as Muscari, Crocus, Iris reticulata and Hyacinth rather than tall Tulips or Daffodils. Plant the bulbs after putting in the bedding plants in autumn.

As already mentioned above, all-over bedding (see page 42) remains the favoured scheme despite the advantages of part bedding. In winter colour can be provided in an all-over bedding scheme by using Universal Pansies, Erica carnea, Polyanthus 'Crescendo' etc. In spring the old stand-by group of Bellis, Polyanthus and bulbs is often used. The summer show is generally a kaleidoscope of colour, but many experts feel that this is not a good idea. The most successful schemes are usually simple ones in which the contrast is with the wall (bright flowers next to pale walls, pale ones next to dark walls) rather than between the plants themselves.

PLANTS FOR PERMANENT PLANTING

Dwarf Berberis	Hebe
Dwarf Conifers	Hedera
Erica	Lysimachia
Euonymus fortunei	Miniature Roses
Glechoma	Vinca

PLANTS FOR SEASONAL PLANTING

Alyssum	Dwarf Lathyrus
Dwarf Antirrhinum	Lobelia
Begonia	Mesembryanthemum
Bellis	Mimulus
Dwarf Bulbs	Pelargonium
Campanula isophylla	Petunia
Cineraria	Polyanthus
Convolvulus	Salvia
Dianthus	Tagetes
Fuchsia	Thunbergia
Gazania	Tropaeolum
Helichrysum	Universal Pansy
Impatiens	Verbena

The clean white lines of the window ▷
*box are unbroken by the planting
display. The tiered arrangement of
bedding plants is strictly upright —
good in a modern and formal setting*

◁ *Geranium, Glechoma, Callistephus and
Felicia combine to make an informal
grouping of upright and pendent plants.
The window box is partly hidden*

△ *Here the window box is completely hidden by the hanging
display of Geraniums. Useful where you want minimum
window cover and maximum wall cover*

CONTAINER TYPE:
HANGING BASKET

About one in three gardens has at least one hanging basket — a spectacular increase on the position just a few years ago. Doorways and walls everywhere are now brought to life in summer, and no other garden feature of similar size can have such a dramatic effect. The hanging basket shares a number of features with the window box — plants are grown well above ground level and trailing plants are especially important. There are some differences, however — the planting area of a hanging basket is usually strictly limited and the most popular approach is to cover the sides as well as the top with leaves and flowers.

Most baskets are bought ready-planted, usually on impulse in spring when colourful displays can be seen hanging up in garden centres everywhere. A word of warning — don't buy a planted-up basket before late May–early June. Many garden centres will plant up your hanging basket for you, but it is quite a simple job to plant your own. The first step, of course, is to obtain an empty basket. At one end of the scale you can buy a complete kit containing basket, liner, bracket and compost — at the other extreme you can make your own from wood strips, kitchen utensils etc. Buying one is the usual course and there are several types from which to choose — the best one for you will depend on the sort of display you have in mind and the time you have available for watering.

Next, choose a suitable site — the usual spot is either close to the front door or on the wall above the patio. For most plants the ideal place is a partly sunny location, which means avoiding north- and south-facing walls. Also keep clear of sites exposed to strong winds or where the basket can be bumped into by passing traffic.

You must ensure that the hook or wall bracket is secure. A well-watered container may weigh 25 lb (11 kg) or more so fix the attachment properly. Remember that brackets fitted with pulleys and baskets with spring-loaded holders are available these days to make raising and lowering the container a simple job. Brackets need not be purely practical — you can find many types which are highly decorative in their own right.

The attraction of a hanging basket is easy to understand — a living ball of beautiful plants can be created to transform a dull wall or plain porch all summer long. You may be tempted to have baskets all over the place, but do remember that a lot of work is involved. Not at the preparation and planting stage — it is watering and trimming of a traditional hanging basket which takes so much time. A basket without a waterproof exterior will need watering daily in summer.

Linings

An open basket needs a liner to retain the compost. Sphagnum moss is the traditional one — the natural look is an advantage but rapid water loss is a problem. There are several types of shaped liners available — some (e.g recycled wool and plastic foam) are good insulators and a few are preformed to fit standard baskets. All allow planting into the sides of the container.

SPHAGNUM MOSS

PLASTIC SHEETING

COCONUT FIBRE

RECYCLED WOOL

BITUMEN PAPER

PLASTIC FOAM

PREFORMED COMPRESSED FIBRE

Types

OPEN BASKETS

OPEN BASKETS have sides as well as a top which are available for planting. When the plants are in full growth the whole structure is covered, so this is the type to choose for maximum display. The open sides mean, however, that without a waterproof liner the compost will dry out quickly — another drawback is that drips after watering can mark the surface below

TRADITIONAL BASKET

The wire basket is the most popular form — once the iron was galvanised or enamelled to protect it from rust but now it is usually plastic-coated. The popular shape is hemispherical, but flat-bottomed ones are easier to fill. Diameters range from 10–16 in. (25–40 cm) — choose the 14 in. (35 cm) size

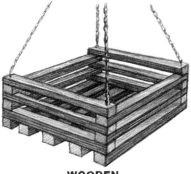

WOODEN BOX

This slatted structure is decorative in its own right. It is generally bought in kit form but you can make one quite easily with hardwood slats. A liner is essential — sphagnum moss or a sheet of brown plastic is a popular choice. The suspended wooden box is more popular for indoor use than outdoors

BIRDCAGE BASKET

A novelty which is frowned upon by some purists but it does have the distinct advantage of providing supports for climbers. Plastic-coated wire is the construction material and both round and hexagonal models are available. Use sphagnum moss plus a polythene sheet liner — see page 28

CLOSED BASKETS

CLOSED BASKETS have a number of advantages. No liner is required and both filling and planting up are generally easier than with open baskets. Even more important is the presence of drip trays or self-watering systems in many models. There is one major drawback — the sides of the standard plastic and terracotta baskets cannot be planted and so a living ball effect is much harder to achieve

SOLID-WALL BASKET

This is not really a basket at all — it is a suspended pot or bowl. The plastic or terracotta sides can look bare until trailing plants grow downwards to partly cover the surface. A few models are available with side planting holes. Look for a solid-wall basket with a drip tray which is either built in or can be clipped on

SELF-WATERING BASKET

A boon for the gardener who cannot water the basket every day in hot weather. Several models are available — the basic principle is a water reservoir at the base together with capillary matting below the compost. The matting is kept constantly wet by the reservoir so that you only need to water once every 1–2 weeks

FIBRE BASKET

Very simple — nothing more than a deep pot of resin-bonded cellulose fibre suspended from 3 metal chains. It has a more natural look than the standard plastic baskets, and holes can be cut in the sides to allow planting as in an open basket. Unfortunately it is not long-lasting and has no drip tray

Filling & Planting

STEP 6:
PLANT UP THE TOP OF THE BASKET
Plant up the centre of the basket with upright bedding plants — set trailing plants around the edge. Firm the compost around the plants — there should be a 1 in. (2.5 cm) watering space between the compost surface and the top of the basket

STEP 7:
WATER THE BASKET
Water in the plants thoroughly but gently. Let the plants settle and start to grow actively before placing outdoors. Ideally the basket should be kept in the greenhouse or near a sunny window for about 2 weeks before being set outside. Harden off if necessary

STEP 5:
FINISH FILLING THE BASKET
Add more compost until the basket is nearly full. Press down gently with your fingers to compact the growing medium — this will reduce the speed of drying

STEP 3:
INSERT THE LINER
Line the basket with a ½–1 in. (1.25–2.5 cm) layer of moist sphagnum moss. Place thin plastic sheeting over this layer and trim away any material which is above the top of the basket. Put a saucer at the bottom to hold the liner down and also to act as a water-holding reservoir

STEP 4:
START TO FILL THE BASKET
Half-fill the basket with moist soilless potting compost. Press down gently and then make 3–5 slits in the plastic at the compost surface level. Through each slit push a young trailing plant so that the soil ball rests on the compost and the top of the plant lies outside the basket

STEP 2:
CHOOSE THE LINER
A liner is required inside the basket in order to hold the compost. You will find several types at the garden centre — see page 26 for examples. Most liners are flat, and are designed to fit a specific size of wire basket. Some come as two semi-circular pieces — others with cut flanges like the petals of a flower. A lining of sphagnum moss is attractive but it is much better to use the sphagnum moss + plastic sheeting system. Proceed to Step 3

STEP 1:
GET THE BASKET READY FOR FILLING
Filling a solid-wall basket is a simple matter. Just place a few crocks above any drainage holes which may be present and then add a soilless potting compost — soil-based composts are too heavy. Omit the crocking step with self-watering and fibre baskets. Firm the compost and go on to Step 6. With a traditional wire basket the situation is more complex. Begin by standing the round-bottomed container in a large pot or bucket for support. Go on to Step 2

STEP 8:
FOLLOW THE AFTERCARE RULES
As with all containers the compost within the basket must not be allowed to dry out. Watering open baskets without a waterproof liner may be necessary every day in summer — watering a solid-wall basket with a drip tray will be required 2–3 times a week. Gently fill the watering space above the compost and allow to drain. Use steps to reach the basket if it cannot be reached from the ground, or use one of the gadgets described in the Watering section in Chapter 5.

Start to feed with a liquid fertilizer 6 weeks after planting. Repeat every 2 weeks or as instructed. Add a slow-release fertilizer to the compost if you want to be spared the trouble of regular repeat feeding. Trim regularly to keep the plants in check and to remove dead blooms. If necessary peg down shoots with hair pins pushed through the lining and into the compost

Plants

The usual pattern is for the basket to be planted up with a variety of summer-flowering bedding plants and then it is placed outdoors in late May or early June. Open baskets have a central planting of compact upright types and a ring of trailing plants around the outer edge. Other trailers are set into the sides — with closed baskets the planting of the sides is omitted.

For summer display the big six are Geranium, Fuchsia, Lobelia, Petunia, Impatiens and Begonia. These plants can be seen everywhere in all sorts of combinations, but the list of bedding plants which will grow in a hanging basket is much, much larger. Use the list on pages 43–51, and do consider some of the newer ones such as Scaevola, Diascia, Petunia 'Surfinia' and Convolvulus sabatius. For something even more unusual you can bed out some of the hardier house plants such as Setcreasea, Zebrina and Ficus pumila, or you can grow Tomatoes (for example 'Tumbler' or 'Tiny Tim') and Strawberries such as 'Alexandria' and 'Aromel'. Many herbs (Sage, Chives, Parsley, Thyme, Tarragon etc) will grow quite happily in a hanging basket.

These out-of-the-way uses are for the adventurous — for the average gardener a hanging container is used for a riot of mixed colours from a variety of bedding plants. Listed below is a selection of bedding plants which have proved their worth in a sunny or partly sunny situation. In a shady spot the choice is much more limited — Mimulus, Impatiens, Ivy, Erica and Bedding Begonia are suitable. The kaleidoscope of colour is not the only approach — growing a single species is often preferable, especially if the basket is small.

In October or November the display is hit by frost and so the basket is emptied and brought indoors to wait for next year's summer display. Garden books sometimes point out that this is a shame as it is during the winter months that colour is most needed at the front of the house. For a winter display you can pick from Universal Pansy, Erica carnea, Bedding Daisy and Variegated Ivy. A word of warning — in a hard winter the compost may freeze solid, so always use a large basket and fit it with a liner with good insulating properties.

PLANTS FOR THE HANGING BASKET

Asarina	Heliotropium
Asteriscus	Impatiens
Begonia	Lantana
Bellis	Dwarf Lathyrus
Brachycome	Lobelia
Calceolaria	Lotus
Calendula	Mimulus
Campanula	Nemesia
Chlorophytum	Nierembergia
Cineraria	Osteospermum
Coleus	Pelargonium
Convolvulus	Petunia
Dianthus	Phlox
Diascia	Portulaca
Euonymus fortunei	Scaevola
Felicia	Tagetes
Fuchsia	Thunbergia
Gazania	Tradescantia
Glechoma	Tropaeolum
Hedera	Verbena
Helichrysum	Viola & Pansy

In recent years the Impatiens ball has become extremely popular. A wire basket is planted with one or more varieties of Busy Lizzie for a summer-long sphere of flowers ▷

◁ The traditional style of hanging basket. A mixture of upright and pendent bedding plants is used to provide a wide assortment of leaf shapes, flower sizes and colours

△ The hanging basket need not be an assortment of varieties and colours. In many situations a solid mass of a single colour can be more dramatic, as these yellow Pansies show

*For many people the single-coloured ▷
basket is too plain and the
kaleidoscope of hues is too bright.
The answer is a subtle blend of
analogous colours — see page 98
for details*

◁ *Something different. In the traditional basket
there is either a ball-like or tumbling effect
— here Thunbergia is used in a closed basket
to produce a distinctly upright arrangement*

△ *Despite everything the professional garden designers may say about
the beauty of single-colour and mixed pastel arrangements, the
bright multicoloured basket remains the firm favourite*

CONTAINER TYPE:
WALL MOUNTED

The wall-mounted container is closely related to the hanging basket. There are both open and closed types, their plant-holding capacity is limited and they are supported above the ground. The basic difference is the method of support — the hanging basket is suspended from above but the wall-mounted container is attached from the side.

In most cases the container is screwed directly on to the wall but there are a few examples where there is a bracket attachment. The wall-mounted container is useful where there is not enough room for a hanging basket, but the small amount of compost which is held by the average model means very frequent watering and the use of plants which can stand occasional dryness.

A liner is essential for the open-sided version — you can use the sphagnum moss + plastic sheeting system outlined on page 28 or you can buy a proprietary preformed type designed to fit the basket.

WALL POT
Many types are available — plain or ornate, small or large. Plastic and terracotta are the usual materials, and attachment is generally by means of a screw

SWALLOW'S NEST POT
A variant of the wall pot — a novelty with a high back and a semi-conical container. The amount of compost is very small, so use it for succulents such as Sedum

PERFORATED WALL POT
Another variant of the wall pot — the sides are perforated so that they can be planted as if it was an open container. Can be highly decorative, but small capacity remains a problem

WALL TROUGH
A better choice than a pot as the capacity is greater — the Apta model illustrated is 24 in. (60 cm) long and 8 in. (20 cm) deep. Plastic, terracotta and reconstituted stone troughs are available

SELF-WATERING WALL TROUGH
Wall-mounted containers need frequent watering — the self-watering version requires watering only at 1–2 week intervals. Can be attached to a fence or under a sill as a window box

HAYRACK CONTAINER
The hayrack or manger is made out of strip metal coated with white or black plastic for rust protection. Attractive in the right setting — use a sphagnum moss + plastic sheeting liner

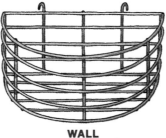

WALL BASKET
This container is half a hanging basket with some type of wall attachment instead of supporting chains. Fill and plant as for a hanging basket — see pages 28 and 29 for instructions

SUSPENDED WALL BASKET
This one differs from the other examples by being circular. The metal basket is supported on a wall-mounted bracket and is planted up like a hanging basket. The container can be rotated

The so-called wall-mounted ▷
container is not always attached to
a solid surface. Here a pair of plastic
wall pots filled with Polyanthus are
attached to iron railings

◁ *This deep horse manger or hayrack with a*
chicken wire liner is used to house a group
of Geraniums. The simplicity of the floral
display ensures that it is the container which
is the focal point

△ *Wall-mounted containers are sometimes used as an alternative to*
window boxes — these open plastic models filled with Impatiens
'Rose Gem' and Ivy provide spots rather than a line of interest

CONTAINER TYPE:

TOWER

With most containers the plants are set into the horizontal surface of the compost at the top of the pot, urn, trough, window box etc. Some planting into the sloping sides of hanging baskets and wall-mounted containers may take place.

With a tower the plants are set into the vertical sides of the container so that an upright column of flowers, fruit or herbs is produced — this column may be round, square or rectangular in outline.

Several proprietary tower containers can be bought from garden centres or by mail order — they usually come as units for stacking on top of each other although the suspended tube made of plastic sheeting has appeared in recent years. The cheapest and sometimes the most satisfactory way of creating a tower in the garden is to make your own from chicken wire and stakes. Drive the stakes into the ground and attach the chicken wire with staples as shown below. Line the inside with polythene sheeting or sphagnum moss and fill with compost, planting up the sides as you go. The final step is to plant up the compost at the top.

Watering poses a problem with all towers — it is essential to ensure that the plants at the bottom of the structure receive an adequate supply. With the chicken wire tower the best plan is to put a shallow layer of small stones at the base and then insert a piece of plastic tubing in the middle, supporting it with compost during the filling process. This tube should have a series of holes drilled at intervals and it should be filled with small stones. Pour water into the tube as well as over the compost surface each time you water.

CUBE TOWER
Illustrated here is the Grow Dice system — plastic cubes filled with a rock-wool compost and bearing 4 planting holes on each side. Support poles are available if required

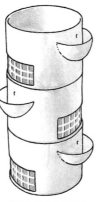

PLASTIC POT TOWER
The first type of tower to become popular — a series of perforated plastic tubes with planting pockets are fitted together to form a column — main use is for Strawberries

PLASTIC BAG TOWER
Several types are available, ranging from simple polythene tubes which are stapled at the bottom to the Flower Tower shown above with a built-in water bowl

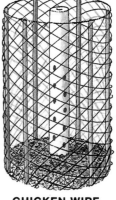

CHICKEN WIRE TOWER
Use a litter basket or make your own out of chicken wire (see above). A miniature version for inserting into a large plant pot or tub can be made in the same way

CONTAINER TYPE:
GROWING BAG

Growing bags have revolutionised the way we grow Tomatoes and Cucumbers under glass. Once the plants went into pots or the border soil but now most greenhouse vegetables are grown in these plastic pillows filled with compost. More than 10 million are sold every year for this purpose.

For several reasons they are much less popular for use outdoors. The bag is generally printed with garish pictures and wording, and staking can be tricky. Waterlogging can be a problem in wet weather.

Despite these points there is a place for growing bags outdoors. The plastic can be hidden by enclosing the bag with bricks or wooden boards and covering the surface with shredded bark — several proprietary growing bag holders are available. Staking systems of various types have been introduced and so have automatic watering systems. The main use for growing bags is where the person without a garden wants to grow Tomatoes, Lettuce or Strawberries on a balcony or in a courtyard — after vegetables a display of bedding plants can be grown. An alternative use for growing bags is to provide a long line of bedding plants at the edge of the patio without going to the expense of buying a number of troughs.

Always shake the bag to loosen the compost before planting. Do read and carefully follow the manufacturer's instructions. Before replanting in the following season turn over the compost surface and add a little fresh material. After the second season of use spread the compost in the garden or add to the compost heap.

If you like to try new things you can use the Grow-pot system. A double plastic pot is pushed into the growing bag — the plant and liquid feed go into the compost-filled central pot and water is applied to the outer ring. The risk of overwatering is reduced.

CONTAINER TYPE:
CONVERTED

In nearly every case the containers we use have been specially made for the purpose and have been bought from a garden centre, DIY store, local shop or a mail order company. The converted container is quite different — it is an object or utensil which was not designed to hold plants but has been used with or without alteration as a receptacle for compost in which plants are grown.

Some of the more popular sorts of converted container are shown on this page but there are many more to be seen — coal scuttles, chamber pots, cisterns, ceramic bowls, bird cages and so on. Take care — not all household bric-a-brac is suitable and some require adaptation before use. Drainage holes at the base are necessary and these are not always possible to create. In addition some form of anti-corrosion treatment may be required.

Two types of converted container shown here illustrate this need for adaptation. Old kitchen sinks can be turned into attractive troughs which look and weather like stone by treating with hypertufa — 1 part cement, 1 part sand and 1 part fine peat blended to a moist mix with water. Coat the sink with a bonding agent and leave to become tacky before painting on the hypertufa mix. When dry paint with yoghurt to promote lichen and moss development. The old tyre is another throwaway product which can be transformed into a container. Cut lengthways through the middle of the tread with a hacksaw — lift up one side to form the bowl of the 'urn' and pull down the other half of the tyre to form the pedestal. Paint black, brown or grey.

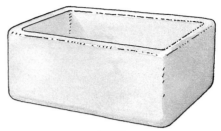

SINK

An old sink with plug removed makes an excellent trough for alpines. In a garden filled with converted containers the white surface may be acceptable — but hypertufa treatment (see introduction on this page) will improve its appearance

OLD TYRES

Two or three old tyres placed on top of each other have long been used as a converted container — sometimes painted white but it is preferable to leave unpainted or to choose a dull and dark coating. Try the urn conversion — see the introduction

CHIMNEY POT

A great favourite over the years in cottage gardens — do not paint or 'improve' in any way. They look best as a group of short and tall ones. Sometimes used as a pot holder

WHEELBARROW

The brightly painted wheelbarrow overflowing with bedding plants is a common sight outside country pubs. An old wheelbarrow can make an attractive container, but it is best left unpainted

TREE STUMP

Rounds cut from a large dead tree can be used as rustic containers. Char the inside with a blowlamp and line with plastic sheeting — pierce the plastic at the base in several places to allow drainage

The good and the bad way to use ▷
old car tyres as containers. In the
foreground is the recommended
'rubber-urn' described on page 36
— in the background is the white-
painted tyre stack which is so often
an eyesore

◀ *A piece of a felled tree trunk has*
been hollowed out and drainage
holes have been bored through
the base. A good choice for the
path or patio near a shrub border
— the insulation against winter
frost is excellent

△ *This boat display is one for the local council and definitely not for the*
average garden, but it does show that large objects as well as kitchen
utensils, bottles, chamber pots etc can be used as converted containers

CONTAINER TYPE:
RAISED BED

It may seem strange to include raised beds in a book on containers because they are usually large and are fixed to the ground, but a grand urn cemented to a brick pier is also large and equally immovable.

The patio is the favourite place for a raised bed, where it adds another dimension and extra splash of colour. The shape, size and material should be matched to the locality. You can use brick, stone, reconstituted stone blocks, logs or railway sleepers — unprotected wood should be painted with a plant-safe preservative. There is a minimum size (18 in. x 18 in. x 18 in.) if the soil is not to dry out too quickly.

Ideally a raised bed should be close to a source of water and the centre will be in reach without having to step on to the surface. The surround should be firm and level and the walls will be really rigid. A few weep holes (small gaps between the building units) should be provided if mortar-bonded bricks, blocks or stones are the building material. During construction hardy rockery perennials can be planted into gaps in the walls — such planting is easy and especially attractive when peat blocks, logs or dry (mortarless) walling is used.

Once the walls of the raised bed have been built the bottom half should be filled with a layer of rubble, stones or broken bricks. Cover this drainage layer with grit and then add a suitable planting mixture (page 7). Use a special mix if rockery perennials are to be grown — see page 69.

The choice of plants is, of course, up to you but a few guidelines may help. A central dot plant may be an attractive feature but a large patch of tall and upright plants can look ungainly. The best choices are generally a range of bushy plants and prostrate ones, with trailers at the edge to drape over and soften the bare faces of the raised bed.

CONTAINER TYPE:
POT HOLDER

A group of ordinary clay plant pots can look quite at home on the flagstones of a cottage garden, but would be rather out of place on the neat patio or close to the formal porchway of a typical garden of today.

In order to hide a pot or pots you can bury them in a compost-filled container — this in-pot planting technique is illustrated on page 23. Alternatively you can put the pot or pots in an empty container — this outer container is called a **pot holder**. The pot holder must be weather-resistant and some form of drainage is necessary. With solid types there should be drainage holes at the base — ordinary wire or lacy pot holders are free-draining along the sides as well as at the base.

The phrase 'pot holder' includes units for holding troughs, growing bags etc as well as pots. Most are decorative, including chimney pots which are sometimes used to hold clay pots. Some, however, are purely practical, such as the drainpipe pot holder.

CACHEPOT
A large pot of terracotta, glazed earthenware, cast aluminium, lead, wood etc designed to hold a planted-up pot. The advantage is that a specimen can be removed and replaced without root disturbance

MULTIPOT HOLDER
A pot holder may house more than one pot. The usual form is a trough — this may be a simple plastic container or an ornate one made of reconstituted stone, fibreglass or lace-like aluminium

DRAINPIPE POT HOLDER
This unit hardly qualifies as a container, although it is certainly a pot holder. It is purely practical rather than decorative — the plastic ring is attached to the drainpipe and a pot is supported by it

GROWING BAG HOLDER
A useful 'pot' holder — the decorative sides improve the appearance of the bag, the base serves as a water reservoir and it may contain or have holes for some form of support

TROUGH HOLDER
This type of holder is used to support a trough above the ground — the favourite materials are plastic-coated wire or cast aluminium. Appears in some catalogues as a planter or jardiniere

HANGING POT HOLDER
This holder has a hanging basket appearance but there are basic differences — the plants are left in their pots and it is suspended by one chain rather than three. A wall-mounted version is available

CHAPTER 3
PLANTS FOR CONTAINERS

After taking a walk along a suburban street you could be forgiven for thinking that only a limited number of plants can be used for growing in containers. Your walk in spring would reveal some but not all free-standing pots and tubs filled with popular bulbs such as Daffodils, Tulips and Hyacinths. Here and there you would see Wallflowers, Pansies, Polyanthus and some double Daisies. A number of the window boxes will contain the same range of plants, but hanging baskets would be an uncommon sight.

Things would be quite different in summer. From June onwards a multitude of pots, troughs, tubs, urns, hanging baskets and window boxes brim over with ever-popular bedding plants you can buy anywhere — Geraniums, Fuchsias, Begonia, Lobelia, Impatiens and so on. In winter, however, nearly all of the hanging baskets will be gone and most of the window boxes will be bare. Sprinkled along the street you would find containers filled with a limited range of plants — Universal Pansies, Ivy, Box and some conifers, but for most containers this is a season of rest.

All this means that the majority of container gardeners pick from the same limited group of plants each year and ignore the vast range of alternatives. It is true that the favourite ones have earned their popularity because they are so reliable and colourful, but it is worth being a little more adventurous. As shown on the next page there are ten main types of container plant, headed of course by bedding plants. This group deserves to be popular, but there is no reason why you should not try some of the less usual ones such as Lotus, Lantana etc.

The role of bedding plants is to provide plant material for seasonal or temporary planting — the floral display lasts for a period of weeks or months and when it is over the plants are removed. The popular bulbs are used for seasonal planting in the same way.

Permanent planting in a free-standing container or window box is seen less often, and usually consists of a specimen tree or shrub in a tub. By choosing the right plant the year-round effect can be striking, and permanent planting should certainly be more widely used for focal points, door and porch decoration etc. If you have a large container to fill it is an excellent idea to include both types of planting — a part seasonal and part permanent display. A permanent skeleton is created with dwarf conifers and evergreen shrubs or perennials, choosing some with bright or variegated foliage for winter colour. In late spring or early summer an assortment of bedding plants is set out to bring a splash of bright hues to the greens and yellows of the permanent planting. In autumn the spent summer bedders are taken out and replaced by bulbs and biennials for the spring display. As a general but by no means universal rule seasonal plants with proper care do better in a container than in the open garden, but permanent plants fare less well.

By the time you reach the end of this chapter you will realise just how many plants can be grown in containers. In addition to the ornamental ones mentioned so far there are rockery perennials, ferns, border perennials, aquatics and Roses. Not all container plants are ornamentals — food plants including fruit as well as vegetables and herbs can be grown.

So many plants, but it would be wrong to assume that *all* garden plants are suitable for the pot or tub on the patio. Prickly and poisonous plants should be avoided, and most tall-growing perennials such as Delphiniums and Red Hot Pokers look out of place. Ornamentals with a short flowering season and foliage plants with straggly growth and uninteresting leaves generally make poor container plants, and so do many vigorous woody types such as fast-growing conifers, Rambler Roses and Apples on non-dwarfing rootstocks.

You are still left with innumerable types from which to choose, and do try to choose well. Pick the appropriate group or groups from the table on page 41 and make sure the varieties are right for the situation — think of the aspect, amount of sunlight, plant height and spread, container type etc. Now look for really good planting material. You can be excused for choosing bargain plants if you have a large bed or border to fill and money is short, but there can be no reason for buying second-best plants if you have just one or two containers to fill.

Main Types

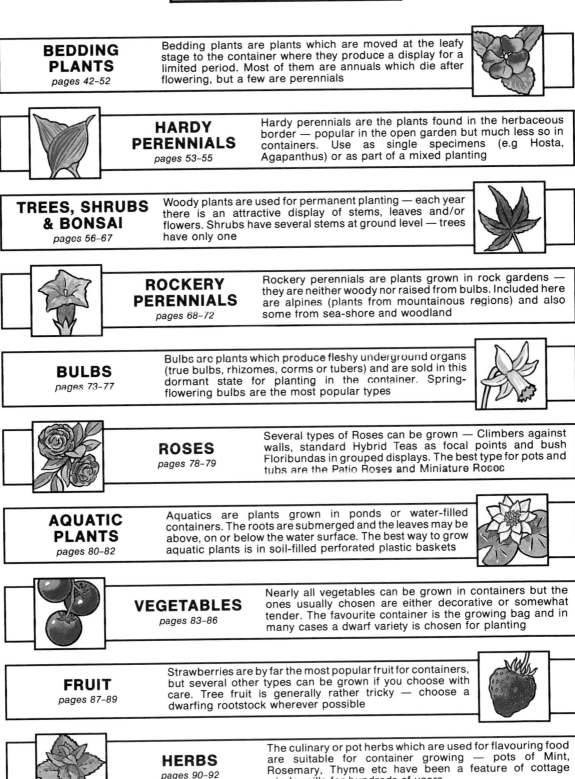

BEDDING PLANTS
pages 42–52

Bedding plants are plants which are moved at the leafy stage to the container where they produce a display for a limited period. Most of them are annuals which die after flowering, but a few are perennials

HARDY PERENNIALS
pages 53–55

Hardy perennials are the plants found in the herbaceous border — popular in the open garden but much less so in containers. Use as single specimens (e.g Hosta, Agapanthus) or as part of a mixed planting

TREES, SHRUBS & BONSAI
pages 56–67

Woody plants are used for permanent planting — each year there is an attractive display of stems, leaves and/or flowers. Shrubs have several stems at ground level — trees have only one

ROCKERY PERENNIALS
pages 68–72

Rockery perennials are plants grown in rock gardens — they are neither woody nor raised from bulbs. Included here are alpines (plants from mountainous regions) and also some from sea-shore and woodland

BULBS
pages 73–77

Bulbs are plants which produce fleshy underground organs (true bulbs, rhizomes, corms or tubers) and are sold in this dormant state for planting in the container. Spring-flowering bulbs are the most popular types

ROSES
pages 78–79

Several types of Roses can be grown — Climbers against walls, standard Hybrid Teas as focal points and bush Floribundas in grouped displays. The best type for pots and tubs are the Patio Roses and Miniature Roses

AQUATIC PLANTS
pages 80–82

Aquatics are plants grown in ponds or water-filled containers. The roots are submerged and the leaves may be above, on or below the water surface. The best way to grow aquatic plants is in soil-filled perforated plastic baskets

VEGETABLES
pages 83–86

Nearly all vegetables can be grown in containers but the ones usually chosen are either decorative or somewhat tender. The favourite container is the growing bag and in many cases a dwarf variety is chosen for planting

FRUIT
pages 87–89

Strawberries are by far the most popular fruit for containers, but several other types can be grown if you choose with care. Tree fruit is generally rather tricky — choose a dwarfing rootstock wherever possible

HERBS
pages 90–92

The culinary or pot herbs which are used for flavouring food are suitable for container growing — pots of Mint, Rosemary, Thyme etc have been a feature of cottage windowsills for hundreds of years

PLANT TYPE:
BEDDING PLANTS

A bedding plant is a plant which is moved at the leafy stage to the container where it will provide a display for a limited period. Note that this definition describes the particular *use* for and not a specific *type* of plant. A Geranium in the greenhouse is a 'half hardy perennial' — the same specimen in a pot outdoors is a 'bedding plant'. Winter Heather in the border is a 'hardy shrub' — growing in a container for a few months to provide a November–March display makes it a 'bedding plant'.

Bedding plants are ideal for people who want a bright splash of colour and who want to ring the changes each season. Hanging baskets are nearly always filled with bedding plants, and they are the most popular plants for free-standing containers. Young plants are bought in pots, trays or strips, but many can be raised easily from seed and some are available as small plugs for growing on before planting out.

Your container garden should never be empty even if you rely solely on bedding plants. The summer bedding display should be followed in autumn with a planting of spring-flowering bedders (Wallflower, Polyanthus, Myosotis, Bellis etc) in some containers and winter-flowering types (Universal Pansy, Polyanthus 'Crescendo' etc) in others. In The Bedding Plant Expert you will find details and illustrations of these plants together with all of the summer-flowering ones. In this section there are brief details of the popular bedding plants specially recommended for containers, together with a few new ones which are now being offered by some garden centres.

As a general rule it is wise to pick more compact varieties than are used in ordinary bedding and plant them more closely together than you would do in a garden bed. Water regularly, use a high potash (K) fertilizer and dead-head faded blooms to prolong the display. Remember that foliage types such as Ivy, Helichrysum and Perilla can add interest to a floral display. If the container is unusually shallow use sun-loving Daisy-like plants such as Gazania.

ALL-OVER BEDDING

In this style the whole of the compost surface is used for growing bedding plants. A single variety may be grown but it is much more usual to have a varied collection. The standard pattern is to have tall plants at the centre of island containers or at the backs of pots or troughs placed against a wall. For large containers one of the dot plants described in this section can be used, but for more modest pots it is often preferable to choose a tall filler plant such as Calendula. After putting in the filler plants set out any edging plants and then use trailing plants to cover up part of the rim and add depth to the display.

PART BEDDING

A large container can look uncomfortably bare from November to March unless it is used for winter bedding. The range here is limited, so it is often a better idea to have one or more woody evergreens as a central specimen or a scattered skeleton within the container. Typical permanent trees and shrubs include Buxus, Pieris, Skimmia, Euonymus and dwarf conifers. Filler, edging and trailing bedding plants are set out around or between this permanent feature to provide a spring, summer or winter display. Another popular part-bedding scheme consists of bulbs planted between biennial bedding plants for a spring display.

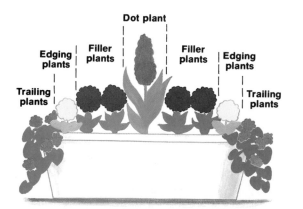

Dot plant

Edging plants | Filler plants | Filler plants | Edging plants

Trailing plants | | Trailing plants

ABUTILON Flowering Maple (HHP) — *Dot*

Ht: 24–36 in. (60–90 cm) *Flowers:* mid June–end Sept

Variegated Leaf Abutilon (A. striatum thompsonii) is grown for its yellow-splashed Sycamore-like leaves. There are several flowering varieties with bell-like flowers — e.g A. hybridum 'Golden Fleece' (yellow) and 'Fireball' (red).

AGERATUM Floss Flower (HHA) — *Filler/Edging*

Ht: 6–18 in. (15–45 cm) *Flowers:* mid June–end Oct

Masses of powder-puff flowers on bushy plants — very popular. For edging choose a compact one such as A. 'Blue Blazer' (blue), 'Pink Powderpuffs' (pink) or 'Summer Snow' (white). Tall ones include 'Tall Blue' and 'Blue Bouquet'.

ALYSSUM Sweet Alyssum (HA) — *Edging*

Ht: 3–6 in. (7.5–15 cm) *Flowers:* mid June–end Sept

A favourite edging plant for window boxes and pots — tiny, honey-scented flowers cover the small-leaved cushions. White is the usual colour — A. 'Snow Drift' etc, but there are also pink ('Rosie O'Day') and red ('Wonderland').

AMARANTHUS Love-lies-bleeding (HHA) — *Dot*

Ht: 24–48 in. (60–120 cm) *Flowers:* mid June–mid Oct

Choose A. caudatus as an eye-catching centrepiece for a big container. The leaves are large and in summer long pendent tassels of tiny red blooms appear. For a change try the red-purple 'Atropurpureus' or the pale green 'Viridis'.

ANTIRRHINUM Snapdragon (HHA) — *Filler*

Ht: 6–18 in. (15–45 cm) *Flowers:* mid June–end Oct

The upright spikes of lipped tubular flowers are known to everyone. There are some tall varieties, but the more compact ones such as A. 'Coronette' are preferable. Dwarfs (6 in.) such as 'Little Gem' are useful for window boxes.

ARCTOTIS African Daisy (HHA) — *Filler*

Ht: 6–18 in. (15–45 cm) *Flowers:* early July–end Sept

Large and showy Daisy-like flowers which open in the sun and close when it is dull. A. speciosa is the yellow-flowering dwarf — much more popular are the multi-coloured mixtures of A. hybrida. A satisfactory choice for a shallow bowl.

ARGYRANTHEMUM Marguerite (HHP) — *Dot/Filler*

Ht: 18–36 in. (45–90 cm) *Flowers:* early June–mid Oct

The popular Marguerite is A. frutescens (Chrysanthemum frutescens) — white Daisies with a yellow centre. Coloured ones are available, such as 'Mary Wootton' (pink) and 'Jamaica Primrose' (yellow).

ASARINA Asarina (HHP) — *Trailing*

Length: 12–36 in. (30–90 cm) *Flowers:* mid June–end Sept

A trailer for hanging baskets or a climber on a support in a pot or trough. You will not find this one in many books but it has begun to appear in some garden centres. The white, pink or purple tubular flowers are borne along the stems.

ASTERISCUS Asteriscus (HHP) — *Filler*

Ht: 12 in. (30 cm) *Flowers:* early June–end Sept

A recent introduction to the container gardening scene. Golden yellow Daisies are borne plentifully above a leafy mound — look for A. maritimus or A. 'Gold Coin'. An excellent choice if you want something different.

Abutilon hybridum

Amaranthus caudatus 'Viridis'

Arctotis hybrida

Argyranthemum frutescens

(HA) Hardy annual · (HHA) Half hardy annual · (HB) Hardy biennial · (HP) Hardy perennial · (HHP) Half hardy perennial

BEGONIA Begonia (HHA or HHP) *Filler/Trailing*
Ht: 4–18 in. (10–45 cm) Flowers: mid June–end Sept
See The Bedding Plant Expert for details. The fibrous-rooted Begonia
(B. semperflorens) is an excellent filler, the large-flowering B. tuberhybrida
makes a useful centrepiece and B. pendula is a hanging basket favourite.

Begonia pendula

BELLIS Daisy (HB) *Filler/Edging*
Ht: 3–6 in. (7.5–15 cm) Flowers: early April–end July
Neat, ground-hugging plants for spring colour. Semi-double and double varieties
are available and the blooms of giant-flowering ones such as B. 'Monstrosa' and
'Goliath' are 2 in. (5 cm) across. Suitable for sun or partial shade.

BRACHYCOME Swan River Daisy (HHA) *Filler*
Ht: 9–15 in. (22.5–37.5 cm) Flowers: mid June–end Sept
Masses of sweetly-scented Daisy-like flowers on wiry stems for a hanging basket.
Not often seen as it is rarely offered by garden centres — you will have to raise it
from seed. Look for B. 'White Splendour', 'Purple Splendour' or 'Blue Star'.

BROWALLIA Bush Violet (HHP) *Filler*
Ht: 9–18 in. (22.5–45 cm) Flowers: end June–end Sept
An unusual plant for hanging baskets with masses of star-shaped tubular flowers
which are 2 in. (5 cm) across. Raise from seed or buy plants from the house plant
section of the garden centre. Not suitable for an exposed site.

Brachycome 'Purple Splendour'

CALCEOLARIA Slipper Flower (HHA) *Filler*
Ht: 9–15 in. (22.5–37.5 cm) Flowers: early June–mid Oct
Small pouched flowers are borne on long stems — the yellow-flowering types are
the only ones you are likely to find. The favourite varieties are C. 'Sunshine' and
'Midas' — the pale-coloured 'Golden Bunch' is more compact.

CALENDULA Pot Marigold (HA) *Filler*
Ht: 9–24 in. (22.5–60 cm) Flowers: mid May–mid Sept
Bushy plants with semi-double or double flowers. Many varieties of C. officinalis
are available — choose a compact one such as C. 'Gypsy Festival' or 'Fiesta' for a
window box. Tall ones include 'Lemon Queen' and 'Art Shades'.

Callistephus 'Miss Europe'

CALLISTEPHUS China Aster (HHA) *Dot/Filler*
Ht: 6–36 in. (15–90 cm) Flowers: mid July–early Oct
Many varieties in nearly all colours have been developed from C. chinensis.
Nearly all are semi-double or double and most look like small Chrysanthemums.
Tall ones such as 'Ostrich Plume' and 'Duchess' can be used as dot plants.

CAMPANULA Trailing Campanula (HHA) *Trailing*
Length: 12 in. (30 cm) Flowers: mid June–early Sept
Many types of Campanula are grown in the garden, but only the trailing types are
recommended for containers. C. isophylla bears starry white or blue flowers —
look for it in the house plant section. C. fragilis is another trailer.

CANNA Indian Shot (HHP) *Dot*
Ht: 24–48 in. (60–120 cm) Flowers: mid July–mid Oct
A real beauty — the large leaves are decorative and the bright blooms are up to
5 in. across. Rhizomes are potted up under glass in March and then bedded out in
June. A large container is necessary. Canna is not suitable for an exposed site.

Canna hybrida

(HA) Hardy annual · (HHA) Half hardy annual · (HB) Hardy biennial · (HP) Hardy perennial · (HHP) Half hardy perennial

CATHARANTHUS Vinca (HHA)   *Filler*

Ht: 6–12 in. (15–30 cm) *Flowers:* early July–end Sept

C. roseus (Vinca rosea) is sometimes listed as Madagascar Periwinkle — a popular plant in the U.S but not in Britain. Phlox-like flowers with a distinct eye are borne above glossy leaves. Raise plants from seed.

CHEIRANTHUS Wallflower (HB)   *Filler*

Ht: 9–24 in. (22.5–60 cm) *Flowers:* mid March–mid June

Yellow is the favourite colour but the varieties range from off white to deep red. Choose C. 'Tom Thumb' if you want a low-growing plant — for May–June blooms grow the orange-flowered Siberian Wallflower.

CHLOROPHYTUM Spider Plant (HHP)   *Dot/Filler*

Ht: 12–18 in. (30–45 cm) *Foliage:* end May–early Oct

This popular house plant makes an attractive centrepiece when it bears arching stems with young plantlets at the tips. Choose C. elatum 'Variegatum' with green and white striped leaves. Prefers partial shade to full sun.

Chlorophytum elatum 'Variegatum'

CINERARIA Dusty Miller (HHA)   *Filler*

Ht: 6–15 in. (15–37.5 cm) *Foliage:* mid May–end Sept

C. maritima (Senecio maritima) is widely used for its ferny silvery-white leaves. This is a compact plant — for a taller variety choose 'White Diamond'. Small yellow flowers appear, but these should be removed at the bud stage.

Cineraria maritima

COLEUS Flame Nettle (HHA)   *Filler*

Ht: 6–18 in. (15–45 cm) *Foliage:* mid June–mid Oct

This plant is grown for its colourful foliage rather than its insignificant blue flowers. Single colour varieties are available — 'Volcano' (red) etc, but multicoloured leaves are more popular. Pinch out tips to induce bushiness.

CONVOLVULUS Convolvulus (HHP)   *Trailing*

Length: 12 in. (30 cm) *Flowers:* mid June–end Sept

The annual C. tricolor (Dwarf Morning Glory) is grown as a bedding plant for the rockery or front of the border. The container Convolvulus is C. sabatius (C. mauritanicus) — a delicate trailing plant with small lavender flowers.

CORDYLINE False Palm (HHP)   *Dot*

Ht: 18–48 in. (45–120 cm) *Foliage:* end May–end Sept

The False Palms are used as single specimens in urns and tubs or as dot plants in mixed plantings. C. australis and C. indivisa bear sword-like leaves on woody trunks — C. terminalis (red-splashed leaves) is more compact.

Coleus blumei

COREOPSIS Tickweed (HA)   *Filler*

Ht: 12 in. (30 cm) *Flowers:* early July–end Sept

The annual forms of Coreopsis bear Marigold-like flowers on stiff stems. The basic colours are yellow, red and brown, and some varieties are bicolours. Choose one of the compact types such as C. 'Dwarf Dazzler'.

DAHLIA Bedding Dahlia (HHA)   *Filler*

Ht: 12–24 in. (30–60 cm) *Flowers:* end June–end Oct

Surprisingly the Bedding Dahlia rarely appears in the lists of plants recommended for containers. This popular bedding plant is easy to grow and the floral display long-lasting. Blooms are single, semi-double or fully double.

Cordyline australis 'Variegata

(HA) Hardy annual · (HHA) Half hardy annual · (HB) Hardy biennial · (HP) Hardy perennial · (HHP) Half hardy perennial

DIANTHUS Dianthus (HA, HB or HHA)   *Filler*

Ht: *6–24 in. (15–60 cm)* **Flowers:** *mid May–end Oct*

See The Bedding Plant Expert. The hybrids of D. caryophyllus (July–Oct) are Annual Carnations, D. chinensis (June–Oct) varieties are Annual Pinks and the varieties of D. barbatus (May–July) are Sweet Williams.

Diascia vigilis

DIASCIA Diascia (HP)   *Filler/Trailing*

Length: *12 in. (30 cm)* **Flowers:** *early June–end Sept*

A newcomer which is becoming popular as a hanging basket plant. The semi-pendent varieties such as D. 'Ruby Field' and 'Pink Queen' form a mat of pale green leaves and lax stems bearing spurred open-faced flowers.

DIMORPHOTHECA Star of the Veldt (HHA)   *Filler*
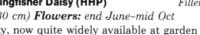
Ht: *6–15 in. (15–37.5 cm)* **Flowers:** *mid June–end Sept*

The value of this South African Daisy is that it will grow in shallow compost and drier conditions than nearly all other bedding plants, but it is not popular as the flowers close in dull weather. The petals surround a central dark disc.

FELICIA Kingfisher Daisy (HHP)   *Filler/Trailing*

Ht: *12 in. (30 cm)* **Flowers:** *end June–mid Oct*

Once a rarity, now quite widely available at garden centres. F. amelloides has straggly stems which makes it useful for hanging baskets — the Daisy-like flowers have narrow blue petals around a golden centre.

Felicia amelloides 'Variegata'

FUCHSIA Fuchsia (HP or HHP)   *Dot/Filler/Edging/Trailing*
Ht: *12–24 in. (30–60 cm)* **Flowers:** *early July–mid Oct*

See The Bedding Plant Expert. Most varieties have bell-like blooms — the rest have tubular flowers. Many bush varieties are available — standard Fuchsias make good dot plants. Trailing types (Basket Fuchsias) are popular.

GAZANIA Gazania (HHA)   *Filler*
Ht: *9–15 in. (22.5–37.5 cm)* **Flowers:** *end June–mid Oct*

This is the most eye-catching of the South African Daisies — the central yellow disc is surrounded by a dark ring and the petals are striped or zoned in bright colours. The largest flowers are borne by G. 'Sundance'.

Fuchsia 'Mrs Popple'

GLECHOMA Ground Ivy (HP)   *Trailing*
Length: *24 in. (60 cm)* **Foliage:** *year round*

A useful foliage plant with pendent stems for hanging baskets or the edges of tubs, troughs etc. G. hederacea 'Variegata' has rounded pale green leaves which are blotched or edged with white. Can be used for winter display.

GOMPHRENA Globe Amaranth (HA)   *Filler*

Ht: *18 in. (45 cm)* **Flowers:** *early July–end Sept*

An unusual plant for a large container — growth is erect and the globular flowers can be cut for drying. There is just one species — G. globosa. A dwarf variety ('Buddy') is available. Not suitable for a shady or exposed site.

GREVILLEA Silk Oak (HHP)   *Dot*
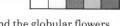
Ht: *Up to 36 in. (90 cm)* **Foliage:** *early June–early Oct*

G. robusta is a house plant which can be used as a centrepiece for a summer container display. It is tree-like and the foliage is graceful and ferny. It will grow in sun or partial shade — staking is necessary.

Glechoma hederacea 'Variegata'

(HA) Hardy annual · (HHA) Half hardy annual · (HB) Hardy biennial · (HP) Hardy perennial · (HHP) Half hardy perennial

HEDERA Ivy (HP)

Trailing

Length: *24 in. (60 cm) or more* **Foliage:** *year round*

Ivy is an easy-to-grow foliage plant for hanging baskets, window boxes etc. There are now many varieties which are more decorative than the ordinary H. helix. The silver-blotched 'Glacier' and yellow-centred 'Goldheart' are examples.

HELICHRYSUM Helichrysum (HHP)

Trailing

Length: *12–36 in. (30–90 cm)* **Foliage:** *end May–early Oct*

H. petiolatum is grown for its attractive display of felted leaves. Silvery-grey is the usual colour, but golden and variegated forms are available. A more compact small-leaved species (H. microphyllum) can be used.

Hedera helix 'Goldheart'

HELIOTROPIUM Heliotrope (HHA)

Filler

Ht: *12–18 in. (30–45 cm)* **Flowers:** *mid June–end Sept*

This old-fashioned bedding plant is used to provide evening fragrance to tubs, hanging baskets and other containers. Tiny flowers are borne in large clusters above dark green corrugated leaves. H. 'Marine' (violet-purple) is popular.

IBERIS Candytuft (HA)

Filler/Edging

Ht: *6–15 in. (15–37.5 cm)* **Flowers:** *mid May–mid Sept*

Each bushy plant bears domed clusters of fragrant flowers — the foliage may be completely covered. Popular choices include I. 'Fairy Mixture' and 'Flash Mixed'. For flowering spikes rather than clusters grow I. umbellata.

IMPATIENS Busy Lizzie (HHA)

Filler/Edging

Ht: *6–18 in. (15–45 cm)* **Flowers:** *early June–mid Oct*

Busy Lizzies have become one of our most popular container plants — see The Bedding Plant Expert. Virtues include continuous flowering and suitability for both sun and semi-shade. Showiest of all are the New Guinea hybrids.

Impatiens 'Super Elfin'

IPOMOEA Morning Glory (HHA)

Dot/Trailing

Length: *up to 8 ft (240 cm)* **Flowers:** *early July–end Sept*

This climber is grown for its large trumpet-like flowers. Train it up a support as a centrepiece or let it trail over the edge of a large container. For a brilliant blue choose I. 'Heavenly Blue' — 'Minibar Rose' is white-edged red.

KALANCHOE Flaming Katy (HHP)

Filler

Ht: *6–18 in. (15–45 cm)* **Flowers:** *mid June–mid Sept*

A well-known house plant which can be used as an unusual container plant. The favourite varieties are the hybrids of K. blossfeldiana with large heads of tiny flowers. Hybrids of K. manginii with bell-like blooms are now available.

Kalanchoe manginii

KOCHIA Burning Bush (HHA)

Dot

Ht: *18–36 in. (45–90 cm)* **Foliage:** *mid May–end Oct*

This plant looks rather like a young conifer — the neat bushy growth is made up of feathery foliage. The favourite one is K. scoparia 'Trichophylla' — a rather tall plant with leaves that turn purple, bronze or bright red in autumn.

LANTANA Yellow Sage (HHP)

Dot/Filler

Ht: *18–30 in. (45–75 cm)* **Flowers:** *mid June–end Sept*

Once a rarity but now offered in early summer by many garden centres. The Verbena-like flower-heads change colour as the flowers mature. Growth is lax — useful for hanging baskets. Standard plants can be used as centrepieces.

Lantana 'Rose Queen'

(HA) Hardy annual · (HHA) Half hardy annual · (HB) Hardy biennial · (HP) Hardy perennial · (HHP) Half hardy perennial

Lathyrus 'Bijou'

Lobelia 'Sapphire'

Lotus berthelottii

Mimulus 'Malibu Ivory'

LATHYRUS Sweet Pea (HP) *Filler/Trailing*
Ht: *6–36 in. (15–90 cm)* **Flowers:** *mid June–mid Sept*
The tall varieties are great garden favourites — the more compact types are used in containers. The so-called Hedge varieties (36 in.) such as L. 'Knee-hi' can be left to trail — Dwarfs (6–12 in.) like 'Patio' are used as fillers.

LAVATERA Annual Mallow (HA) *Dot*
Ht: *24–48 in. (60–120 cm)* **Flowers:** *mid June–end Sept*
A showy and bushy annual which makes a good centrepiece — the trumpet-shaped flowers are 3–4 in. across. Stake tall varieties such as L. 'Sunset'. For more compact growth choose 'Mont Blanc' (white) or 'Ruby Regis' (pink).

LIMNANTHES Poached Egg Plant (HA) *Edging*
Ht: *4 in. (10 cm)* **Flowers:** *early June–mid Oct*
You will have to search for this neat and attractive edging plant which provides a change from Alyssum and Lobelia. The ferny foliage is pale green and the yellow petals of each flower have a distinct white edge.

LOBELIA Lobelia (HHA) *Edging/Trailing*
Ht: *4–6 in. (10–15 cm)* **Flowers:** *mid June–mid Oct*
Lobelia is the No.1 edging and trailing plant for hanging baskets and other containers. Favourite trailing Lobelias include L. 'Sapphire' and 'Blue Basket'. Edging types are bushy — look for 'Crystal Palace' and 'Cambridge Blue'.

LOTUS Coral Gem (HHP) *Trailing*
Length: *24 in. (60 cm)* **Flowers:** *early July–mid Sept*
A conservatory plant which is now being sold for hanging baskets. L. berthelottii bears silvery needle-like leaves along its stems. The 'lobster claw' flowers are red — the variety 'Fire Vine' has orange blooms. Not suitable for cold sites.

LYSIMACHIA Creeping Jenny (HP) *Trailing*
Length: *12 in. (30 cm)* **Flowers:** *early June–end July*
A cottage garden plant which is occasionally used in hanging baskets and window boxes. L. nummularia is a creeping plant which grows only 2–3 in. high but its stems can be invasive. Grow the yellow-leaved compact variety 'Aurea'.

MESEMBRYANTHEMUM Livingstone Daisy (HHA) *Edging*
Ht: *4–6 in. (10–15 cm)* **Flowers:** *mid June–mid Sept*
Now called Dorotheanthus, this carpeting plant is covered by bright and glistening flowers in full sun and a good summer, but it is disappointing in dull weather. Some varieties are bicoloured with a pale-coloured inner zone.

MIMULUS Monkey Flower (HHA) *Filler/Edging*
Ht: *6–12 in. (15–30 cm)* **Flowers:** *early June–mid Oct*
This plant has the opposite needs to the one above — it thrives best in a poor summer as it needs both shade and compost which never dries out. The trumpet-like flowers are spotted or blotched — look for M. 'Calypso' and 'Magic'.

MYOSOTIS Forget-me-not (HB) *Filler/Edging*
Ht: *6–18 in. (15–45 cm)* **Flowers:** *early April–end May*
The traditional blue bedder for spring edging or planting under bulbs. The dwarfs include M. 'Blue Ball', 'Ultramarine' and 'Pink Gem'. If you want taller (12–18 in.) plants choose 'Royal Blue' or the large-flowered 'Blue Bouquet'.

(HA) Hardy annual · (HHA) Half hardy annual · (HB) Hardy biennial · (HP) Hardy perennial · (HHP) Half hardy perennial

NEMESIA Nemesia (HHA)   *Filler*
Ht: 9–12 in. (22.5–30 cm) **Flowers:** *early June–end Sept*
N. strumosa is an old favourite with many varieties and hybrids — you can choose a single colour but the usual plan is to buy a mixture such as 'Carnival' and 'Funfair'. The flowering season is short in a hot summer.

NICOTIANA Tobacco Plant (HHA)   *Filler*
Ht: 12–24 in. (30–60 cm) **Flowers:** *mid June–mid Oct*
Choose one of the modern dwarf hybrids rather than the tall old-fashioned Tobacco Plant. N. 'Crimson Bedder' and the 'Domino' and 'Nikki' series have flowers which do not droop nor do they close during the day.

Nicotiana 'Domino Bo-Peep'

NIEREMBERGIA Cup Flower (HHP)   *Filler/Edging*
Ht: 6–9 in. (15–22.5 cm) **Flowers:** *mid June–end Sept*
Something unusual but well worth growing. The spreading stems are covered by masses of yellow-centred cup-shaped flowers. N. 'Purple Robe' is violet-blue and 'Mont Blanc' is white. Good for pots and hanging baskets.

OSTEOSPERMUM Osteospermum (HHP)   *Filler*
Ht: 12–24 in. (30–60 cm) **Flowers:** *mid June–end Sept*
These Daisy-like plants have become increasingly popular in recent years. The star of the show is O. 'Whirligig' with white/blue petals shaped like spoons — other varieties include 'Buttermilk' (yellow) and 'Nairobi Purple'.

Osteospermum 'Whirligig'

PELARGONIUM Geranium (HHP)   *Dot/Filler/Trailing*
Ht: 6–18 in. (15–45 cm) **Flowers:** *mid June–end Oct*
Quite simply, the Queen of Container Bedders — see The Bedding Plant Expert for details. The Bedding Geraniums are the most popular, but there are also Multibloom, Fancy-leaved, Spreading and the trailing Ivy-leaved Geraniums.

PERILLA Perilla (HHA)   *Dot*
Ht: 24 in. (60 cm) **Foliage:** *early June–end Sept*
P. frutescens is an out-of-the-ordinary foliage plant used as a centrepiece for its purple leaves. Pinch out stem tips when young to induce bushiness. Varieties with convoluted and deeply incised leaves are available.

Pelargonium peltatum 'Roulettii'

PETUNIA Petunia (HHA)   *Filler/Trailing*
Ht: 6–18 in. (15–45 cm) **Flowers:** *mid June–mid Oct*
The showy, funnel-shaped blooms can be seen everywhere in summer. The Multiflora group have 2 in. wide flowers — the Grandifloras are larger but are not borne freely. The new trailing one is P. 'Surfinia'.

PHLOX Annual Phlox (HHA)   *Filler/Edging*
Ht: 6–12 in. (15–30 cm) **Flowers:** *mid June–end Sept*
The old varieties were tall and untidy — choose one of the modern compact or dwarf types. The blooms may have a distinct eye and the flower-heads are about 4 in. across. The petals of P. 'Twinkling Stars' and 'Petticoat' are deeply cut.

PLUMBAGO Cape Leadwort (HHP)   *Dot*
Ht: 36–48 in. (90–120 cm) **Flowers:** *early Aug–end Sept*
Grow it on its own in a container or as a dot plant in the centre of a display — the heads of sky-blue flowers of P. capensis are eye-catching. The variety 'Alba' is white. Provide support for the stems.

Petunia 'Surfinia Purple'

(HA) Hardy annual · (HHA) Half hardy annual · (HB) Hardy biennial · (HP) Hardy perennial · (HHP) Half hardy perennial

Polyanthus variabilis

Scaevola 'Blue Fan'

Schizanthus 'Hit Parade'

Thunbergia alata 'Susie'

PORTULACA Sun Plant (HHA)   *Filler/Edging*
Ht: 4–8 in. (10–20 cm) *Flowers:* mid June–end Sept
A low-growing but wide-spreading succulent for a container in full sun — the bowl-shaped flowers cover the reddish leaves. Look for one which doesn't close its petals in dull weather — P. 'Sundance' and 'Sunglo' are examples.

PRIMULA Primrose (HP)   *Filler*
Ht: 9–12 in. (22.5–30 cm) *Flowers:* early March–end May
By far the most popular type for spring bedding is Polyanthus (P. variabilis). The flowers are generally yellow-eyed and are massed in large heads. Choose P. 'Pacific Giants' for size and 'Crescendo' for winter flowers.

PYRETHRUM Silver Lace (HHP)   *Filler/Edging*
Ht: 4 or 12 in. (10 or 30 cm) *Foliage:* early June–mid Oct
This plant P. ptarmiciflorum (other name : Tanacetum ptarmiciflorum) is grown for its finely-divided foliage which has a feathery appearance — rather similar to but less popular than Cineraria. The leaves are silvery.

RESEDA Mignonette (HA)   *Filler*
Ht: 12 in. (30 cm) *Flowers:* early July–end Sept
This plant is not worth growing for its appearance — growth is untidy and the trusses of tiny flowers have a washed-out look. Reseda is grown for its evening fragrance — use it for an extra dimension in a mixed planting.

SALVIA Salvia (HHA)   *Filler*
Ht: 6–12 in. (15–30 cm) *Flowers:* mid June–end Oct
By far the most popular Salvia is S. splendens (Scarlet Sage) and the favourite varieties are bright red — 'Blaze of Fire', 'Vanguard' etc. 'Tom Thumb' is the dwarf. Red is not the only colour — mixtures such as 'Phoenix' are available.

SCAEVOLA Scaevola (HHP)   *Trailing*
Length: 12 in. (30 cm) *Flowers:* mid June–end Sept
A conservatory plant now offered for hanging baskets. The thick stems are lax and bear Dandelion-like leaves. The flowers are quite distinctive — they have petals on one side only. Look for S. 'Blue Fan' or 'Blue Wonder'.

SCHIZANTHUS Poor Man's Orchid (HHA)   *Filler*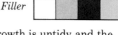
Ht: 6–18 in. (15–45 cm) *Flowers:* early July–mid Aug
The flowers of two annuals are truly exotic — the veined velvety trumpets of Salpiglossis and the multicoloured Orchid-like blooms of Schizanthus. Grow Schizanthus in a peat-based compost.

TAGETES Marigold (HHA)   *Dot/Filler/Edging*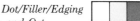
Ht: 6–24 in. (15–60 cm) *Flowers:* mid June–end Oct
A large group — see The Bedding Plant Expert for details. The small-flowered singles are sold as Tagetes — the larger ones include French, Afro-French, American and African Marigolds. T. 'Doubloon' has 5 in. wide blooms.

THUNBERGIA Black-eyed Susan (HHA)   *Trailing*
Length: 48 in. (120 cm) *Flowers:* early July–end Sept
Grow this one up a support as a centrepiece or allow to trail in a window box or hanging basket. The 2 in. wide blooms are funnel-shaped and may have a black centre. Choose the variety T. alata 'Susie'.

(HA) Hardy annual · (HHA) Half hardy annual · (HB) Hardy biennial · (HP) Hardy perennial · (HHP) Half hardy perennial

TITHONIA Mexican Sunflower (HHA)
Dot

Ht: *36 in. (90 cm)* **Flowers:** *mid July–mid Oct*

If you want an out-of-the-ordinary centrepiece and the site is sheltered and sunny then this one is worth trying. The upright stems bear Dahlia-like flowers with yellow-backed orange or yellow petals. Choose T. 'Goldfinger'.

TORENIA Wishbone Flower (HHA)
Trailing

Length: *12 in. (30 cm)* **Flowers:** *early July–end Sept*

This annual is better known as a house plant than an outdoor bedder. The pendent stems of T. fournieri bear tubular flowers which are violet with a dark purple lower lip and a yellow blotch. The variety 'Alba' is all-white.

Torenia fournieri

TROPAEOLUM Nasturtium (HA)
Filler/Trailing

Ht: *6–18 in. (15–45 cm)* **Flowers:** *mid June–mid Oct*

An old favourite for all sorts of containers. As a filler choose 'Jewel Mixture' (semi-double), 'Alaska' (white-speckled foliage) or 'Empress of India' (red). For hanging baskets use the semi-trailing 'Gleam' hybrids.

URSINIA Ursinia (HHA)
Filler

Ht: *12–18 in. (30–45 cm)* **Flowers:** *early July–end Aug*

Yet another bedding plant from South Africa with Daisy-like flowers. Its advantage is that the blooms stay open in cloudy weather, but its disadvantage is that the flowering season lasts for only two months.

VENIDIUM Monarch of the Veldt (HHA)
Dot/Filler

Ht: *12–24 in. (30–60 cm)* **Flowers:** *mid June–mid Oct*

This plant with its Sunflower-like blooms is a good choice for a tub in a sunny spot, but you will have to search to find plants or seed. The 4 in. wide blooms are cream or orange with a prominent purple-black centre.

Tropaeolum 'Dwarf Jewel Scarlet'

VERBENA Verbena (HHA or HHP)
Filler/Trailer

Ht: *6–18 in. (15–45 cm)* **Flowers:** *mid June–mid Oct*

Small Primrose-like flowers are borne in clusters at the top of the stems — a popular choice for pots and window boxes. Some varieties are upright (V. 'Tropic' etc) — others are trailers (e.g 'Springtime').

VIOLA Viola, Pansy (HA or HB)
Filler/Edging

Ht: *6–9 in. (15–22.5 cm)* **Flowers:** *depends on type*

Violas and Pansies are excellent for containers in a number of ways. They will grow in partial shade and they stay in flower for 4–6 months. There are winter-flowering ones such as the V. 'Universal' strain.

Verbena 'Peaches and Cream'

ZEA Ornamental Sweetcorn (HHA)
Dot

Ht: *36–48 in. (90–120 cm)* **Foliage:** *mid June–mid Oct*

A bold centrepiece plant which will remain attractive throughout the season. The upright stems bear gracefully arching leaves which are striped — white, cream, yellow, orange or red depending on the variety.

ZINNIA Zinnia (HHA)
Dot/Filler

Ht: *6–30 in. (15–75 cm)* **Flowers:** *early July–mid Oct*

A Dahlia-like plant which is available in a wide range of heights, colours and flower shapes and sizes — make sure you choose the right one. Z. 'Thumbelina' is a dwarf — 'State Fair' and 'Dahlia-flowered' are giants.

Viola 'Joker'

(HA) Hardy annual · (HHA) Half hardy annual · (HB) Hardy biennial · (HP) Hardy perennial · (HHP) Half hardy perennial

*A classical bedding scheme for an urn ▷
— the central dot plant is Cordyline
australis, Petunias and Calceolarias
are the filler plants and the edging is
provided by Scaevola — a welcome
change from the ever-popular Nemesia*

*◁ You don't have to plant a garish mixture to
attract attention — this pondside display of
Begonia pendula in a terracotta jar is an
effective focal point at the unplanted side of
the pool*

*Despite all that has been ▷
written about dot plants and
about single variety planting,
the mixed colourful mass
remains the most popular
choice and it can certainly light
up a dull area or an all-green
background*

PLANT TYPE:
HARDY PERENNIALS

Hardy perennials are the plants found in the herbaceous border — so popular in the open garden but much less so in containers. The reason for this minor role for so many well-known plants is perhaps easy to understand. The space available in containers is usually strictly limited and we want to achieve maximum impact, so the choice is usually between a bright splash of season-long colour from bedding plants or a pleasing architectural effect from a tree or shrub.

If you want to have a mixed display in a modest-sized container then this popular approach is the right one. If, however, you have a large container to fill with plants then you should seriously consider hardy perennials as part of the scheme. There are two basic ways to use them. Put a single plant such as Hosta or Agapanthus in a pot, or use one or more types as part of a mixed planting scheme in a large container. The annual care programme includes top dressing in spring, feeding in summer and removing dead foliage, stems etc in late autumn. About once every three years it will be necessary to lift and divide vigorous plants and then pot the strongest pieces.

ACANTHUS Bear's Breeches   *Deciduous*
Ht: *36-48 in. (90-120 cm)* **Flowers:** *early July–mid Sept*
A. spinosus is grown for its deeply-divided arching leaves and tall spires of tubular white and purple flowers. The foliage bears spines — A. mollis latifolius is spineless. Acanthus needs space — grow as a specimen plant.

AGAPANTHUS African Lily   *Deciduous*
Ht: *30 in. (75 cm)* **Flowers:** *mid July–early Sept*
Clusters of trumpet-shaped blooms appear on long stems above the strap-like leaves. Needs full sun and protection of crowns with sand or peat in winter. A. 'Headbourne Hybrid' is the hardiest.

Alchemilla mollis

AJUGA Bugle   *Semi-evergreen*
Ht: *4-6 in. (10-15 cm)* **Flowers:** *mid May–mid Aug*
An edging plant which soon spreads to form a leafy carpet. Blue flowers are borne in short spikes, but the main colour comes from the leaves. Choose from all-green, green/cream, green/grey, bronze or red/purple.

ALCHEMILLA Lady's Mantle   *Deciduous*
Ht: *12-18 in. (30-45 cm)* **Flowers:** *mid June–mid Aug*
A. mollis is an old favourite — this ground cover forms a flat-topped clump of foliage with branching sprays of tiny greenish-yellow flowers in summer. The leaves are lobed and saw-edged. Cut back in autumn.

AQUILEGIA Columbine   *Deciduous*
Ht: *18-24 in. (45-60 cm)* **Flowers:** *mid May–end June*
Modern varieties such as A. 'McKana Hybrids' and the 'Music' series are much more colourful than the old-fashioned Columbine. The foliage is ferny and the petals have prominent spurs. Grows in sun or partial shade.

Aquilegia hybrida

Deciduous: Stems/leaves die in winter   *Semi-evergreen: Some stems/leaves die in winter*
Evergreen: Stems/leaves retained over winter

Bergenia cordifolia

Dicentra spectabilis

Doronicum plantagineum

Hemerocallis 'Stafford'

ARTEMISIA Wormwood
Evergreen

Ht: *12–36 in. (30–90 cm)* **Foliage:** *year round*

A group of perennials and sub-shrubs which are grown for their fern-like and aromatic silvery foliage. The flowers are insignificant. Hardy ones include the compact A. pedemontana (12 in.) and 'Powis Castle' (36 in.).

ASTILBE Astilbe
Deciduous

Ht: *12–36 in. (30–90 cm)* **Flowers:** *mid June–mid Aug*

The foliage is ferny and the tiny flowers are carried in large feathery plumes. Tall varieties such as A. arendsii 'Deutschland' make excellent centrepieces in light shade and in peat-based compost.

BERGENIA Bergenia
Evergreen

Ht: *18 in. (45 cm)* **Flowers:** *early March–end April*

A bold and spreading plant which is best grown on its own in the container. The large leathery leaves turn red in autumn and the bell-shaped flowers are borne on branched spikes. Thrives in sun or partial shade.

DICENTRA Bleeding Heart
Deciduous

Ht: *12–18 in. (30–45 cm)* **Flowers:** *early May–mid June*

A good choice if you want a late spring-flowering plant for a shady spot. The leaves are ferny and the locket-shaped flowers are borne on long arching stems. Choose one of the modern hybrids — use peat-based compost.

DORONICUM Leopard's Bane
Deciduous

Ht: *18–36 in. (45–90 cm)* **Flowers:** *mid April–early June*

Doronicum provides a spring display of large Daisy-like blooms. For single flowers choose D. 'Miss Mason' or the taller 'Harpur Crewe'. 'Spring Beauty' is a fully double variety. Provide some support for the stems.

GERANIUM Crane's Bill
Deciduous

Ht: *12–18 in. (30–45 cm)* **Flowers:** *early June–mid Aug*

The true Geranium (not to be confused with the ever-popular bedding 'Geranium') forms clumps of lobed leaves and bears clusters of saucer-shaped flowers. Remove dead blooms — grow in sun or light shade.

GEUM Geum
Deciduous

Ht: *12–18 in. (30–45 cm)* **Flowers:** *early June–mid Sept*

Popular in the border but unusual in containers. Wiry stems bearing bowl-shaped single or semi-double flowers grow above the foliage. The two old favourites are G. 'Mrs Bradshaw' (red) and 'Lady Stratheden' (yellow).

HELLEBORUS Hellebore
Evergreen

Ht: *12–18 in. (30–45 cm)* **Flowers:** *mid Jan–mid April*

The blooms of the Hellebores are a welcome sight in winter or early spring — large open saucers with a central boss of stamens. The Christmas Rose (H. niger) is the early one — the Lenten Rose (H. orientalis) blooms later.

HEMEROCALLIS Day Lily
Deciduous

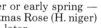

Ht: *24–36 in. (60–90 cm)* **Flowers:** *end June–mid Aug*

Clumps of strap-like leaves give rise to branching flower stalks, each flower lasting a single day. The Lily-like trumpets are available in a wide range of colours. Thrives in sun or light shade.

Deciduous: Stems/leaves die in winter   Semi-evergreen: Some stems/leaves die in winter
Evergreen: Stems/leaves retained over winter

HEUCHERA Coral Flower
Evergreen

Ht: 18–30 in. (45–75 cm) Flowers: mid June–mid Aug

The Maple-like leaves form neat mounds of green or reddish bronze and in summer the slender stems appear, bearing dense clusters of tiny bell-shaped flowers. H. 'Red Spangles' is the brightest variety.

HOSTA Plantain Lily
Deciduous

Ht: 18–30 in. (45–75 cm) Flowers: early July–mid Sept

An excellent dual purpose plant for a container in a shady spot. The range of foliage colours is shown above — the floral spikes bear white or lavender blooms. For deep shade choose an all-green variety.

Hosta 'Ginko Craig'

INCARVILLEA Chinese Trumpet Flower
Deciduous

Ht: 24 in. (60 cm) Flowers: end May–end June

Try this one if you like something different and the container is in full sun. In early summer several large trumpet-like flowers appear on each stalk of I. delavayi, after which the ferny leaves appear.

IRIS Iris
Deciduous

Ht: 12–36 in. (30–90 cm) Flowers: depends on type

The Bulb group is described later — the ones here belong to the Rhizome group with thick, underground creeping stems. The leaves are usually flat and broad. Most are Bearded Irises — see The Flower Expert for details.

Iris pumila 'Bright Eyes'

LAMIUM Deadnettle
Evergreen

Ht: 6 in. (15 cm) Flowers: end April–mid June

There is nothing particularly showy about Lamium — it is a creeping ground cover for a container in shade. The Nettle-like leaves are generally splashed or lined with silver and the tubular blooms are hooded.

PHORMIUM New Zealand Flax
Evergreen

Ht: 36–60 in. (90–150 cm) Foliage: year round

An excellent specimen plant to grow in a large pot in full sun. The tall leaves are sword-like and may be variegated or coloured. Protect from severe frost — the all-green varieties are the hardiest.

PULMONARIA Lungwort
Evergreen

Ht: 6–12 in. (15–30 cm) Flowers: mid March–mid May

A shade lover from the cottage garden — the leaves are spotted with white and the tubular flowers change from pink to blue as they open. Variations are available — all-green leaves and flowers which are red or lavender.

Phormium tenax

SEDUM Ice Plant
Deciduous

Ht: 12–24 in. (30–60 cm). Flowers: mid Aug–mid Oct

The popular border Sedum is the Ice Plant (S. spectabile). The leaves are fleshy and the plate-like flower-heads are made up of tiny flowers. Withstands hot and dry conditions — attractive to butterflies.

STACHYS Lamb's Ear
Evergreen

Ht: 4–18 in. (10–45 cm) Foliage: year round

This perennial is grown for its attractive foliage. S. lanata leaves are covered in white silvery hairs — a welcome touch of brightness in winter. The small lavender flowers on upright spikes in midsummer are insignificant.

Stachys lanata

Deciduous: Stems/leaves die in winter   Semi-evergreen: Some stems/leaves die in winter
Evergreen: Stems/leaves retained over winter

PLANT TYPE:
TREES, SHRUBS & BONSAI

More and more people these days are discovering that containers can be used for trees and shrubs, and not just for bedding plants and bulbs. The basic advantage of these woody types is their great variety of shape, size and colour plus the boon of not having to lift out and replace the plants every year. Because of this latter point trees and shrubs are usually referred to as 'permanent' plants, but this is not strictly true. Every 3–5 years it will generally be necessary to pot on or repot (see page 17) although leaving the shrub alone and adding a top-dressing to the surface may be satisfactory — see Chapter 5.

The first step is to understand the meaning of the words. A *shrub* is a perennial plant which bears several woody stems at ground level — a *tree* on the other hand bears only one mature stem at ground level. Sounds straightforward, but the dividing line between trees and shrubs is not always clear-cut. Several shrubs, such as Holly, may grow as small trees. Some of these trees and shrubs are *deciduous*, losing their leaves in the autumn — the rest are *evergreen*, keeping their foliage in winter. There are two special groups — the *climbers* which can attach themselves to or twine around an upright structure and the *conifers* which are evergreen (nearly always) and bear cones (always).

Catalogues and large garden centres will present you with an extensive and bewildering array of woody plants — consult The Tree & Shrub Expert and Flowering Shrub Expert for details and pictures of all the popular and many not-so-popular ones. The types described on the following pages are the trees and shrubs which have proved their worth in containers. Slow-growing conifers are especially useful as they do not mind root restriction.

A glance through this section will show you that all sorts of shapes and colours are available. There are ground-hugging plants like Juniper and Periwinkle, exotic 'Palms' such as Cordyline, neat bushes like Box and Rhododendron, and weeping trees such as the Kilmarnock Willow. If you can choose only one, perhaps the best selection would be a flowering evergreen with showy blooms and attractive leaves — Camellia and Pieris are good examples.

There are three basic ways to use a tree or shrub in a container. Firstly, you can plant one singly in a pot, tub etc to cover or decorate a wall or other vertical surface (Wall Planting) or you can plant it without a wall backing (Specimen Planting). Finally, you can plant it as part but not all of the planting scheme in the container (Mixed Planting). In all cases you must ensure that the pot is large enough — 18 in. (45 cm) wide and 12 in. (30 cm) deep is the recommended minimum for vigorous woody plants when mature.

At the end of this section is a note on Bonsai — the art of cultivating miniature-sized trees in bowls.

WALL PLANTING
The value of using plants to cover an unsightly or bare wall is well-known — you will see climbers growing directly against house walls or on trellises everywhere. The easiest way to grow these clothing plants is directly in the garden soil, but this is not always possible. Courtyard gardens, apartment balconies and many patios are examples of locations where containers provide the base for wall planting. Many plants can be used — some are natural climbers, such as Vitis and Parthenocissus, and others are shrubs with lax stems (for example Kerria and Forsythia) which need to be tied to wires or trellis work.

SPECIMEN PLANTING

The simplest form of permanent planting is to have a single tree or shrub in the centre of the container. It should provide year-round interest, so choose carefully. Make sure that the colour, shape etc fit in with the background. Regular trimming and annual pruning are often necessary, and never more so than when you are following the age-old craft of topiary. The favourite quintet of topiary plants are Box, Bay Laurel, Yew, Privet and Holly. Geometrical or fanciful shapes are created — wiring is necessary for complex forms. An alternative form of topiary is created by using a shaped frame of chicken wire over which Ivy is grown.

MIXED PLANTING

A mixed planting may consist of several different trees or shrubs, but it is much more usual to have trees and shrubs with other types of plants. The woody plant or plants may dominate the scheme, such as a large Japanese Maple underplanted with small bulbs. In other arrangements the shrubs or trees play a minor part, as when a dwarf conifer or two are used as a background to a large planting of bedding plants in a window box or tub. A few rules. The various plants should need the same cultural requirements — sun or shade, acid or neutral compost etc. Next, a central tree or shrub should not be so vigorous as to swamp the underplanting nor so small as to be masked by the other plants.

Acer palmatum 'Dissectum'

Buxus sempervirens

Calluna vulgaris 'Elkstone'

Camellia japonica

ABIES Fir

Evergreen

Ht: *12–24 in. (30–60 cm)* **Foliage:** *year round*

Most Firs are far too vigorous for container cultivation, but A. balsamea 'Hudsonia' grows very slowly and rarely exceeds 18 in. It is flat-topped — A. arizonica 'Compacta' has the more characteristic cone shape.

ACER Maple

Deciduous

Ht: *up to 72 in. (180 cm)* **Foliage:** *end April–end Oct*

There are many types — the favourite ones are varieties of Japanese Maple (A. palmatum). They are grown for their leaf colour, especially the autumn hues, and their divided leaves. Choose a sheltered spot in light shade.

ARUNDINARIA Bamboo

Evergreen

Ht: *36–48 in. (90–120 cm)* **Foliage:** *year round*

The dwarf Bamboos make good container plants. The popular one is A. viridistriata with yellow-striped grass-like leaves and purplish stems. Grow A. variegata for cream-striped foliage. Partial shade is best.

AUCUBA Aucuba

Evergreen

Ht: *48 in. (120 cm)* **Foliage:** *year round*

A popular garden shrub which will grow in shade. The favourite varieties have variegated leaves — the most widely grown is A. japonica 'Variegata' which has oval glossy leaves splashed with yellow blotches.

BERBERIS Barberry

Deciduous

Ht: *24–36 in. (60–90 cm)* **Foliage:** *end April–early Nov*

There are evergreen species but it is the deciduous types which are usually chosen. They have colourful leaves and bright berries. The basic species is B. thunbergii — yellow, bronze, purple and red varieties are available.

BUDDLEIA Butterfly Bush

Deciduous

Ht: *48–60 in. (120–150 cm)* **Flowers:** *mid July–mid Sept*

The garden shrub Buddleia is not often grown in containers but is worth considering for a large tub. Pick a variety of B. davidii — the cone-shaped floral spikes are very large. Prune properly — see The Flowering Shrub Expert.

BUXUS Box

Evergreen

Ht: *48 in. (120 cm) or more* **Foliage:** *year round*

The Common Box (B. sempervirens) is the most popular one — there are compact and variegated varieties. Box produces masses of small, glossy leaves and withstands regular clipping. Never let compost dry out.'

CALLUNA Heather

Evergreen

Ht: *9–24 in. (22.5–60 cm)* **Flowers:** *early July–end Nov*

A host of Common Heather (C. vulgaris) varieties are available for flowering in summer or autumn. Many have colourful foliage — gold, grey, bronze, red or purple. Always use an ericaceous compost — trim over in March.

CAMELLIA Camellia

Evergreen

Ht: *48–60 in. (120–150 cm)* **Flowers:** *early Dec–mid May*

An excellent plant for a large tub — oval glossy leaves all year round and large, showy blooms in winter or spring. Choose a variety of C. japonica or C. williamsii — early- and late-blooming varieties are available. Protect from morning sun.

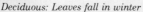

Deciduous: Leaves fall in winter   *Evergreen: Leaves retained in winter*

CHAMAECYPARIS False Cypress
Evergreen

Ht: up to 72 in. (180 cm) **Foliage:** *year round*

C. lawsoniana is grown everywhere, but you must choose one of its dwarf varieties for a container — examples are 'Minima Aurea' (yellow) and 'Ellwoodii' (grey-green). C. pisifera 'Boulevard' (steel-blue) is widely grown.

CHOISYA Mexican Orange Blossom
Evergreen

Ht: up to 48 in. (120 cm) **Flowers:** *mid April–end May*

A good specimen plant — the rounded bush is densely clothed with glossy foliage and a mass of fragrant starry flowers in spring. C. ternata is the usual species — the yellow-leaved variety 'Sundance' is more eye-catching.

CLEMATIS Clematis
Evergreen or Deciduous

Ht: up to 72 in. (180 cm) **Flowers:** *April or July*

The popular large-flowering varieties are difficult to grow in containers, but there are two types which do well. C. armandii is a vigorous evergreen with white and pink varieties — C. florida 'Sieboldii' bears Passion Flower-like blooms.

Chamaecyparis pisifera 'Plumosa'

CONVOLVULUS Shrubby Bindweed
Evergreen

Ht: 12–18 in. (30–45 cm) **Flowers:** *mid May–mid Aug*

C. cneorum is not often seen in gardens, but it is a good container plant. The bush bears silvery leaves and in May the pink buds begin to open into white trumpets. Not as tender as the textbooks suggest.

CORDYLINE Cabbage Palm
Evergreen

Ht: up to 72 in. (180 cm) **Foliage:** *year round*

Cordylines have already been dealt with as bedding plants — see page 45. One of them (C. australis) is hardy enough to be grown as an outdoor Palm-like tree. The long leaves may be green, purple ('Purpurea') or red ('Rubra').

Choisya ternata 'Sundance

DEUTZIA Deutzia
Deciduous

Ht: 36–48 in. (90–120 cm) **Flowers:** *early May–end July*

This graceful shrub is seen at its best when grown as a specimen plant away from other subjects. When given room the plant is covered with masses of small bell-like flowers in summer. Single and double forms are available.

ELAEAGNUS Oleaster
Evergreen

Ht: 36–48 in. (90–120 cm) **Foliage:** *year round*

One variety of this vigorous foliage shrub is popular as a tub plant. E. pungens 'Maculata' has spiny stems and its leathery leaves are splashed with bright yellow. Cut back each spring to keep in bounds.

Cordyline australis 'Purpurea'

ERICA Heather
Evergreen

Ht: 9–30 in. (22.5–75 cm) **Flowers:** *depends on type*

See The Flowering Shrub Expert for details. Types are available for flowering at any season, but the early-flowering ones are the best sorts for containers. Use ericaceous compost for lime-hating varieties.

EUCALYPTUS Gum Tree
Evergreen

Ht: up to 60 in. (150 cm) **Foliage:** *year round*

E. gunnii is the one to grow. It is pruned back to just a few inches in May to maintain its shrub form and the distinctive juvenile foliage — round and waxy blue-green. Keep in full sun.

Elaeagnus pungens 'Maculata'

Deciduous: Leaves fall in winter   *Evergreen: Leaves retained in winter*

Euonymus radicans
'Silver Queen'

Fuchsia 'Marinka'

Hydrangea macrophylla

Ilex altaclarensis 'Lawsoniana'

EUONYMUS Euonymus
Evergreen

Ht: up to 60 in. (150 cm) Foliage: year round

A useful foliage plant with all-green or variegated leaves — E. japonicus varieties are taller than the more popular E. radicans (E. fortunei) types. Allow to spread. Trim into neat shapes or grow against a wall.

FATSIA Fatsia
Evergreen

Ht: 60 in. (150 cm) Foliage: year round

F. japonica is a showy specimen plant with large, deeply-lobed leaves borne on long leaf stalks. There is a type ('Variegata') with white-edged foliage. White candelabra-like flower-heads appear in October.

FORSYTHIA Forsythia
Deciduous

Ht: 24–72 in. (60–180 cm) Flowers: early March–end April

Not one of the best container plants, but worth growing as a herald of spring if you do not have a garden. Grow a variety of F. suspensa for wall planting or one of the forms of F. intermedia as a specimen bush.

FUCHSIA Fuchsia
Deciduous

Ht: 18–60 in. (45–150 cm) Flowers: mid July–mid Oct

Fuchsias have already been dealt with as bedding plants — see page 46. There are a number of hybrids and varieties which are classed as hardy — F. magellanica is the most popular species. Cut back stems in April.

HEBE Shrubby Veronica
Evergreen

Ht: 12–48 in. (30–120 cm) Flowers: mid May–mid Nov

You will find many sorts of this shrubby evergreen at any large garden centre — see The Tree & Shrub Expert for details. A few have scale-like leaves, others have oval foliage. Some bear small flowers in bottle-brush spikes.

HEDERA Ivy
Evergreen

Ht: 24 in. (60 cm) or more Foliage: year round

Hederas have already been dealt with as bedding plants — see page 47. However, all these varieties of H. helix are hardy and are widely used as climbers or trailers in permanent planting schemes. Good in sun or shade.

HYDRANGEA Hydrangea
Deciduous

Ht: 36–48 in. (90–120 cm) Flowers: mid July–end Sept

One of the best of all late summer container plants. The favourite ones are the Mopheads or Hortensias with large globular heads. The Lacecaps have flat heads. Use ericaceous compost if you want to have blue flowers.

HYPERICUM St. John's Wort
Evergreen

Ht: 18–36 in. (45–90 cm) Flowers: mid June–mid Oct

An easy plant with large Buttercup-like flowers — thrives in sun or partial shade. Prune in spring. The usual choice is H. calycinum but there are better forms. H. moserianum 'Tricolor' has green/cream/pink leaves.

ILEX Holly
Evergreen

Ht: up to 72 in. (180 cm) Foliage: year round

Too well-known to need description, but there are types with spineless leaves, black berries etc. To ensure berry production on a specimen plant choose a self-fertile one such as I. aquifolium 'Pyramidalis'.

Deciduous: Leaves fall in winter   Evergreen: Leaves retained in winter

JUNIPERUS Juniper   *Evergreen*
Ht: 6–48 in. (15–120 cm) **Foliage:** *year round*

One of the most important of the container conifers. There are a number of suitable types, such as J. communis 'Compressa' (conical), J. horizontalis (carpeting) and J. virginiana 'Skyrocket' (columnar).

Juniperus horizontalis

KERRIA Jew's Mallow   *Deciduous*
Ht: up to 72 in. (180 cm) **Flowers:** *early April–end May*

This well-known garden shrub is not often grown in containers, but it can be used for wall planting in sun or partial shade. Choose K. japonica 'Pleniflora' and train the stems against wires or on trellis. Prune in June.

LAURUS Bay Laurel   *Evergreen*
Ht: up to 72 in. (180 cm) **Foliage:** *year round*

Laurus is widely used as a tub plant, clipped and trimmed into neat geometric shapes. The main shaping should take place in mid spring and late summer. Not a trouble-free plant — damage by frost and scale insects are common.

LAVANDULA Lavender   *Evergreen*
Ht: 12–36 in. (30–90 cm) **Flowers:** *early July–end Aug*

Old English Lavender (L. spica or L. officinalis) is an old favourite with grey-green leaves and blue flowers. For something different look for flowers which are white ('Nana Alba') or pink ('Hidcote Pink').

Laurus nobilis

LIGUSTRUM Privet   *Evergreen*
Ht: up to 72 in. (180 cm) **Foliage:** *year round*

The ordinary all-green, yellow or variegated Privet is used everywhere for hedging — the role of Privet in containers is to serve as a topiary plant. Choose a small-leaved type such as L. delavayanum or ionandrum.

MAGNOLIA Magnolia   *Evergreen*
Ht: 48–60 in. (120–150 cm) **Flowers:** *early March–end April*

There are many beautiful Magnolias but only one is recommended for tub culture. The Star Magnolia (M. stellata) forms a compact bush and in spring the narrow-petalled starry flowers appear. Choose a sheltered spot.

NANDINA Heavenly Bamboo   *Evergreen*
Ht: 36–48 in. (90–120 cm) **Flowers:** *early June–end July*

This up-and-coming evergreen has one great virtue as a container plant — it changes with the seasons. Its green leaves are flushed with red in spring and with orange in autumn. White summer flowers turn to red autumn berries.

Magnolia stellata

PARTHENOCISSUS Virginia Creeper   *Deciduous*
Ht: up to 240 in. (600 cm) **Foliage:** *end April–mid Nov*

The bright red autumn leaves of this clinging vine are a familiar sight on houses, and it can be used for wall planting in a tub. The basic type P. tricuspidata has all-green leaves in summer — P. henryana has variegated foliage.

PASSIFLORA Passion Flower   *Deciduous*
Ht: up to 180 in. (450 cm) **Flowers:** *mid June–mid Sept*

A vigorous climber — provide support. The blooms are large and unusual — orange egg-shaped fruits appear in autumn. P. caerulea is a rather tender white variety — P. umbilicata is violet. Grow against a south or west wall.

Nandina domestica

Deciduous: Leaves fall in winter   *Evergreen: Leaves retained in winter*

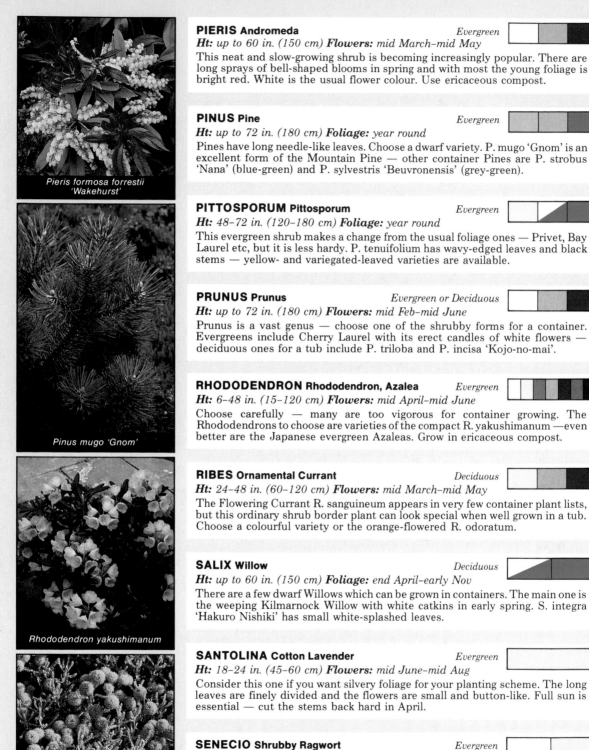

Pieris formosa forrestii 'Wakehurst'

Pinus mugo 'Gnom'

Rhododendron yakushimanum

Santolina chamaecyparissus

PIERIS Andromeda
Evergreen

Ht: up to 60 in. (150 cm) *Flowers: mid March–mid May*

This neat and slow-growing shrub is becoming increasingly popular. There are long sprays of bell-shaped blooms in spring and with most the young foliage is bright red. White is the usual flower colour. Use ericaceous compost.

PINUS Pine
Evergreen

Ht: up to 72 in. (180 cm) *Foliage: year round*

Pines have long needle-like leaves. Choose a dwarf variety. P. mugo 'Gnom' is an excellent form of the Mountain Pine — other container Pines are P. strobus 'Nana' (blue-green) and P. sylvestris 'Beuvronensis' (grey-green).

PITTOSPORUM Pittosporum
Evergreen

Ht: 48–72 in. (120–180 cm) *Foliage: year round*

This evergreen shrub makes a change from the usual foliage ones — Privet, Bay Laurel etc, but it is less hardy. P. tenuifolium has wavy-edged leaves and black stems — yellow- and variegated-leaved varieties are available.

PRUNUS Prunus
Evergreen or Deciduous

Ht: up to 72 in. (180 cm) *Flowers: mid Feb–mid June*

Prunus is a vast genus — choose one of the shrubby forms for a container. Evergreens include Cherry Laurel with its erect candles of white flowers — deciduous ones for a tub include P. triloba and P. incisa 'Kojo-no-mai'.

RHODODENDRON Rhododendron, Azalea
Evergreen

Ht: 6–48 in. (15–120 cm) *Flowers: mid April–mid June*

Choose carefully — many are too vigorous for container growing. The Rhododendrons to choose are varieties of the compact R. yakushimanum —even better are the Japanese evergreen Azaleas. Grow in ericaceous compost.

RIBES Ornamental Currant
Deciduous

Ht: 24–48 in. (60–120 cm) *Flowers: mid March–mid May*

The Flowering Currant R. sanguineum appears in very few container plant lists, but this ordinary shrub border plant can look special when well grown in a tub. Choose a colourful variety or the orange-flowered R. odoratum.

SALIX Willow
Deciduous

Ht: up to 60 in. (150 cm) *Foliage: end April–early Nov*

There are a few dwarf Willows which can be grown in containers. The main one is the weeping Kilmarnock Willow with white catkins in early spring. S. integra 'Hakuro Nishiki' has small white-splashed leaves.

SANTOLINA Cotton Lavender
Evergreen

Ht: 18–24 in. (45–60 cm) *Flowers: mid June–mid Aug*

Consider this one if you want silvery foliage for your planting scheme. The long leaves are finely divided and the flowers are small and button-like. Full sun is essential — cut the stems back hard in April.

SENECIO Shrubby Ragwort
Evergreen

Ht: 24–36 in. (60–90 cm) *Flowers: mid June–end Sept*

Like Santolina this shrub is grown for its foliage rather than its yellow flowers and it needs full sun. The oval leaves have silvery hairs and the Daisy-like flowers are borne in clusters. Choose S. 'Sunshine'.

Deciduous: Leaves fall in winter   *Evergreen: Leaves retained in winter*

SKIMMIA Skimmia   *Evergreen*

Ht: 24–36 in. (60–90 cm) **Foliage:** *year round*

This rounded shrub should be more widely grown. The oval leaves are leathery and in spring there are large clusters of tiny white flowers. Bright red berries appear in autumn on female plants if a male variety is nearby.

TAXUS Yew   *Evergreen*

Ht: 24–60 in. (60–150 cm) **Foliage:** *year round*

Nearly all Yews are slow-growing and make good specimen plants in a container. Grow T. baccata 'Fastigiata' for a dark green narrow column or 'Fastigiata Aureomarginata' for yellow-edged leaves. Caution — Yew is poisonous.

THUJA Arbor-vitae   *Evergreen*

Ht: 12–60 in. (30–150 cm) **Foliage:** *year round*

This conifer has branches covered with scale-like leaves. There are several dwarf varieties — examples include T. occidentalis 'Rheingold' (bronze), 'Holmstrup' (green) and T. orientalis 'Aurea Nana' (yellow).

TRACHYCARPUS Fan Palm   *Evergreen*

Ht: up to 72 in. (180 cm) **Foliage:** *year round*

This is the only True Palm which can be expected to live outdoors in Britain, and this only applies to sheltered and mild sites. The large fan-like leaves are borne at the top of a thick trunk. Move indoors in winter if possible.

VINCA Periwinkle   *Evergreen*

Ht: 4–12 in. (10–30 cm) **Flowers:** *mid April–mid Sept*

Vinca is a useful sub-shrub for ground cover or the edge of the container. It will grow in sun or shade and the flowering season is unusually long. V. minor is smaller and less invasive than V. major.

VITIS Ornamental Vine   *Deciduous*

Ht: 240 in. (600 cm) or more **Foliage:** *mid April–early Nov*

Several varieties of the ordinary Grape Vine are grown for their leaves rather than fruit — the stems climb by means of tendrils. V. vinifera 'Brandt' has green leaves which turn red in autumn — the red leaves of 'Purpurea' turn purple.

WEIGELA Weigela   *Deciduous*

Ht: 36–48 in. (90–120 cm) **Flowers:** *mid May–end June*

An easy shrub for sun and partial shade with masses of open bells in late spring. There are various leaf and flower colours — examples include W. florida 'Variegata' (pale pink; white-edged leaves) and W. 'Bristol Ruby' (red).

WISTERIA Wistaria   *Deciduous*

Ht: 150 in. (375 cm) or more **Flowers:** *early May–mid June*

A glorious climbing shrub which can be grown in a large pot or tub in full sun. The Pea-like flowers are borne in long chains — W. floribunda 'Macrobotrys' is a good choice. See The Flowering Shrub Expert for pruning notes.

YUCCA Yucca   *Evergreen*

Ht: 24–48 in. (60–120 cm) **Flowers:** *early July–end Aug*

Many books sing the praises of Yucca on the patio with its sword-like leaves and large flower-heads, but take care with varieties such as Y. gloriosa which have sharp tips. Yucca is a slow starter.

Skimmia japonica

Weigela florida

Wisteria sinensis

Yucca gloriosa 'Variegata'

Deciduous: Leaves fall in winter   *Evergreen: Leaves retained in winter*

The leaf colour and architectural shape of this Acer palmatum 'Dissectum' are effective, but it is the sharp contrast with the all-green background which makes this display so outstanding as a focal point ▷

◁ Topiary can be simple in shape like the clipped Box on page 58 or it can be ornate as with this Picea albertina growing in a wooden tub. Eye-catching perhaps, but trimming may be both tricky and time-consuming

A popular way to use a ▷ tree to decorate the front door. The pot-grown Bay Laurel provides year-round interest and the bedding plants below provide seasonal colour. Note the colour link with the window box

Climbers can often be left
unsupported in tall containers so
as to grow as trailing plants. This
specimen of Clematis 'Marie
Boisselot' has clothed both the
terracotta jar and surrounding area
with its pure white flowers

◁ A standard tree can be used to add height
and crowning interest to a group of
containers. Don't be afraid of choosing the
unusual — this Salix integra 'Hakuro Nishiki'
is a Willow with reddish stems and white-
splashed leaves

△ Sunlight can be an ingredient of good design when displaying trees
in pots. Clever positioning of these coppery-leaved Cordylines has
produced a dramatic pattern of shadows below the glistening foliage

Bonsai

Well-grown bonsai always create a great deal of interest wherever they are seen — in gardens, shows or garden centres. Gnarled trunks, windswept branches and tiny leaves — each specimen a perfect miniature of the same tree growing in nature.

This miniaturisation is not achieved by choosing naturally dwarf varieties nor by simply keeping the plant in a small pot and leaving it there to cramp the roots. The starting point is an ordinary tree which is known to respond to the bonsai technique, and with patience and skill it is cultivated and trained to produce one of the traditional growth forms shown on the next page.

The official definition sets out the technique in a nutshell. A bonsai is "a tree encouraged to conform in all aspects with ordinary trees, except for its miniature size. The technique consists of keeping the tree confined to its pot by pinching out the top growth and pruning the roots to strike a balance between the foliage above and the roots below, and at the same time to develop a satisfactory shape".

Bonsai on offer for sale will usually be about 4 years old. During the early training period the plant will have been kept in a pot and every 1–2 years both root and stem pruning will have taken place. In addition the branches will have been trained into attractive shapes with stiff 'bonsai wire'. When the bonsai was 3–4 years old it will have been transferred into a bonsai bowl.

There is no such thing as a 'bargain' bonsai. A specimen which seems surprisingly inexpensive is either an attractively shaped but untrained seedling or a mature plant of a naturally dwarf variety. If you have the time and patience you can grow your own true bonsai. Pot up a seedling or rooted cutting of one of the plants suggested on page 67 — use a 3 in. (7.5 cm) pot filled with a soil-based compost. Add extra sand if a conifer is to be grown. When the main stem has reached the desired height pinch out the growing point. Remove some of the lower branches and pinch out the tips of upper side branches. After 2 years repotting is necessary and so is root pruning — in spring remove the plant from the pot and cut away about ⅓ of the roots. Replant in a bonsai bowl. During the growing season continue to pinch out growing tips, remove unwanted growth, train branches with bonsai wire and cut off sun-scorched leaves. Carry out the repotting and root pruning process every 2 years.

Keep compost moist at all times — daily watering may be necessary. Provide some protection to prevent the compost being baked by hot summer sun or frozen solid in winter. Bonsai can be brought indoors, but outdoor varieties can be kept inside for only 4–5 days at a time. Mist daily during the stay indoors.

There are some bonsai (Ficus, Punica, Acacia, Sagaretia, Bougainvillea etc) which are not hardy. Treat them as above in summer — keep indoors during the winter.

Acer palmatum

Pinus densiflora

PLANTS

The favourite subjects for classical bonsai are conifers — the leaves are generally small and evergreen, and the plants are remarkably long-lived. Popular types include:

Abies koreana
Cedrus deodara
Chamaecyparis pisifera
Cryptomeria japonica
Juniperus chinensis
Larix decidua

Larix kaempferi
Picea brewerana
Pinus nigra
Pinus sylvestris
Thuja plicata
Tsuga canadensis

Many other deciduous and evergreen trees and shrubs can be grown as bonsai. Some of the well-known ones are:

Acer palmatum
Acer platanoides
Betula pendula
Carpinus betulus
Chaenomeles speciosa
Crataegus oxyacantha
Fagus sylvatica
Fraxinus excelsior
Laburnum anagyroides

Magnolia stellata
Malus (fruiting varieties)
Prunus (flowering varieties)
Pyracantha angustifolia
Quercus rubra
Rhododendron (Azalea varieties)
Rosa (Patio varieties)
Salix babylonica
Wisteria sinensis

SHAPES

FORMAL UPRIGHT

INFORMAL UPRIGHT

TWIN TRUNK

SLANTING

WINDSWEPT

WEEPING

CASCADE

SEMI-CASCADE

ROOT-OVER-ROCK

PLANT TYPE:
ROCKERY PERENNIALS

In the garden centre and general plant catalogue you will often find a large group of plants grouped together as **alpines**. Here you will see many familiar residents of most rockeries — Sedum, Saxifrage, Alyssum saxatile and so on. Not all of the plants in the rockery or in this section of the garden centre are alpines, however, because this term properly refers to those compact herbaceous or sub-shrubby plants which were originally collected from mountainous regions such as the Alps and Himalayas. A much better name for this group is **rock garden plants** — included here are the alpines together with some alpine-like plants collected from both sea-shore and woodland. In addition many of the specimens you will find on the 'alpine' bench at your garden centre have no natural home — they are man-bred hybrids.

The examples listed in the following A–Z section are **rockery perennials** which are not woody nor raised from bulbs, but amongst the rock garden plants you will see in the well-stocked rockery are also dwarf bulbs, dwarf shrubs, dwarf conifers and ferns.

The traditional home for these plants is the rockery or rock garden — these terms are interchangeable. The rock garden, however, is not for everyone — it takes time, trouble and money to build and needs to be at least 8 ft (240 cm) x 4 ft (120 cm) to be really worthwhile. Where space is limited a good alternative for a rock garden plant collection is a raised bed or trough. In both cases the plants are raised above ground level for greater enjoyment and easier maintenance. The containers are also filled with a special planting mixture (see page 69) rather than ordinary soil.

The basics of raised bed construction are outlined on page 38 — fill it with the alpine planting mixture described on page 69. A raised bed made by the dry-stone wall method has the advantage of allowing a range of rock garden plants to be grown in the cracks between the blocks or stones — the easiest construction unit to use is the reconstituted stone block. A wall above 1 ft (30 cm) high will need a 6 in. (15 cm) foundation of rubble or concrete.

The raised bed made by the dry-stone wall or more usual mortar-bonded block method should be filled to within 2 in. (5 cm) of the top and allowed to settle before planting up with specimens of various shapes, sizes and colours. Cover the soil with a 1 in. (2.5 cm) layer of stone chippings — the use of larger stones between the plants is a matter of personal taste but they are an aid to plant growth.

Using a stone trough or old sink means rock garden plants can be grown anywhere, including on a patio or balcony. Some difficult alpines which often rot outdoors can survive the winter in the excellent drainage provided by a deep trough. For filling and planting instructions see page 69.

Filling & Planting an Alpine Trough

STEP 6:
FOLLOW THE AFTERCARE RULES
Regular watering will be necessary in hot and dry weather during the growing season, but do avoid overwatering. Water until it is seen to run out of the drainage hole or holes, but wait until the top inch or two of the planting mixture is dry before rewatering. Winter can be a difficult time for the alpine trough garden. Delicate types can be protected by placing a sheet of glass over them, using bricks to support the glass above the plants. Do not put up this protection until the cold weather arrives and remove it as soon as the weather turns mild in spring

STEP 5:
PLANT UP THE CONTAINER
Draw up your plan on paper and begin planting up a couple of weeks after filling the trough. Begin with a conifer or two, such as the upright Abies balsamea 'Hudsonia' and the spreading Juniperus 'Depressa Aurea'. Next, put in mat- or cushion-forming plants between the stones — examples include Draba and Morisia. Now fill in with other rockery perennials taking care not to choose quick-spreading invaders for small containers and not to set the plants too closely together. Finally, plant some trailers to grow over the edge of the trough. Water in immediately even if rain is forecast. Cover all bare soil with a 1 in. (2.5 cm) layer of stone chippings

STEP 4:
ADD ROCKERY STONES
Landscape the surface with 2–4 stones — try to find ones which are deeply fissured and lichen-covered. Partly bury each stone to $\frac{1}{3}$–$\frac{1}{2}$ of its depth and aim to make the stones look like an outcrop. You can use tufa (see page 11) for this purpose and grow a plant or two in the rock itself

STEP 3:
ADD THE PLANTING MIXTURE LAYER
Make up the planting mixture. A standard alpine mix which is suitable for nearly all rockery perennials is made by blending 1 part topsoil, 1 part peat or well-rotted leaf mould and 1 part grit or stone chippings. If you plan to grow mainly lime-hating plants then a better mix is 1 part topsoil, 2 parts sphagnum peat and 1 part lime-free gravel or pea shingle. Firm down the planting mixture with your hands as you add it to the trough — fill it to within 1 in. (2.5 cm) of the top and leave to settle

STEP 2:
PUT THE DRAINAGE LAYER IN PLACE
The ideal time to fill and plant an alpine trough is late spring, although any time from mid spring to early autumn will do. Late autumn or winter planting should be avoided as the plants will have no time to become established before the onset of bad weather. Before filling cover the drainage hole or holes with large crocks (broken plant pots) or similar material — make sure that water runs freely through the crocked hole. Now add a 2 in. (5 cm) layer of gravel or rubble

STEP 1:
PUT THE CONTAINER IN PLACE
The ideal container for a miniature alpine garden is either a stone farmyard trough or deep sink, but such objects are hard to find these days. A satisfactory alternative is either a reconstituted stone trough with a rough rustic finish or an old glazed sink which has been covered with hypertufa (see page 36). Whichever container you choose must have adequate drainage. The first step is to place it on firm supports in a sunny spot. Bricks or blocks are the usual form of support and these should lift the trough well above the ground. If bricks are more than three high they should be bonded together with mortar. Sinks generally have the drainage hole on one side — slope the container slightly when placing it on the supports so that the hole is at the lower end

Alyssum 'saxatile

Androsace sarmentosa
'Salmons Variety'

Dianthus alpinus

Draba aizoides

AETHIONEMA Aethionema
Evergreen

Ht: 6 in. (15 cm) Flowers: end May–mid Aug

A. 'Warley Rose' is a shrubby plant which bears rounded clusters of rosy red flowers for many weeks in a sunny spot. The succulent grey leaves form a dense carpet which spreads to about 12 in. (30 cm).

ALYSSUM Gold Dust
Evergreen

Ht: 8 in. (20 cm) Flowers: mid April–mid June

Over-popular, perhaps, but still attractive. A. saxatile bears tiny bright yellow flowers which cover the greyish leaves. Cut back after flowering — it can be invasive. Dwarf varieties include 'Tom Thumb' and 'Compactum'.

ANDROSACE Rock Jasmine
Evergreen

Ht: 4–6 in. (10–15 cm) Flowers: end April–early June

Grey or green leaves — spreading, cushion-forming or trailing depending on the species. All bear tiny, Primrose-like flowers. The popular one is A. sarmentosa with wide-spreading rosettes of leaves. A. carnea is a cushion type.

ARMERIA Thrift
Evergreen

Ht: 3–8 in. (7.5–20 cm) Flowers: mid April–end July

The common Thrift is A. maritima — mounds of grassy leaves and ball-like flower-heads on long stalks. Pink, white and red varieties are available. For early flowering and stemless flowers choose the dwarf A. caespitosa.

ASPERULA Alpine Woodruff
Evergreen

Ht: 1–4 in. (2.5–10 cm) Flowers: end May–end June

The Alpine Woodruff forms prostrate mats of tiny leaves — the green-leaved ones are easier to grow than the woolly ones. The pink tubular flowers are borne in clusters — look for A. lilaciflora or A. gussonii.

AUBRIETA Rock Cress
Evergreen

Ht: 3–5 in. (7.5–12.5 cm) Flowers: mid April–mid June

A great favourite in rockeries but too invasive for many containers — cut back hard after flowering. The grey-green downy leaves are covered by the flat-faced flowers — many varieties and variegated leaves available.

CAMPANULA Bellflower
Deciduous

Ht: 3–10 in. (7.5–25 cm) Flowers: mid June–mid Aug

Masses of bell-shaped flowers are the key feature of the Campanula species, but there is a compact one (C. garganica) which bears starry blooms. The most popular species is C. carpatica with erect 2 in. wide flowers.

DIANTHUS Rockery Pink
Evergreen

Ht: 2–8 in. (5–20 cm) Flowers: end May–mid Aug

The Rockery Pinks form neat cushions or spreading carpets of grey or green mossy foliage. These leaves are covered by the sweet-smelling and generally fringed flowers. Miniatures include D. alpinus and D. freynii.

DRABA Whitlow Grass
Evergreen

Ht: 2–4 in. (5–10 cm) Flowers: early April–early May

D. aizoides has greyish leaves borne in rosettes which are clustered together to form a bristly cushion. The flowers are carried on wiry stems. Another yellow Draba is the even more compact D. bryoides imbricata.

Deciduous: Stems/leaves die in winter   Evergreen: Stems/leaves retained over winter

DRYAS Mountain Avens — *Evergreen*
Ht: 2–4 in. (5–10 cm) Flowers: mid May–mid June

D. octopetala is a European wild flower. The creeping woody stems hug the ground and in late spring the flowers appear — Rose-like with 8 petals and a yellow centre. The summer seed-heads are silky.

Dryas octopetala

ERODIUM Storksbill — *Deciduous*
Ht: 2–6 in. (5–15 cm) Flowers: end May–mid July

A number of clump-forming species are available for growing in containers. The single saucer-shaped flowers are prominently veined. E. corsicum is a mat-forming type — check that the one you choose is hardy.

GENTIANA Gentian — *Evergreen*
Ht: 3–9 in. (7.5–22.5 cm) Flowers: depends on type

The first choice when looking for a blue alpine. There are many varieties — spring-, summer- or autumn-flowering and hard or difficult depending on the species. See The Rock & Water Garden Expert.

GERANIUM Rockery Cranesbill — *Deciduous*
Ht: 6 in. (15 cm) Flowers: mid May–mid Aug

These low-growing perennials produce divided or lobed leaves in spring and bowl-shaped, veined flowers in summer. G. cinereum is an attractive species — popular varieties are 'Ballerina' and 'Lawrence Flatman'.

Gentiana acaulis

HELIANTHEMUM Rock Rose — *Evergreen*
Ht: 4–8 in. (10–20 cm) Flowers: mid May–mid July

The spreading wiry stems are covered with a sheet of colour during the summer months. Each flower lasts a day or two, but new ones are borne in profusion. Once the first flush has faded cut the stems back hard.

HUTCHINSIA Chamois Cress — *Evergreen*
Ht: 2 in. (5 cm) Flowers: mid May–mid July

A number of the plants listed here are old favourites which you can buy from any garden centre, but H. alpina is an out-of-the-ordinary one. It produces clusters of white flowers on compact leafy rosettes.

LEWISIA Lewisia — *Evergreen*
Ht: 9–12 in. (22.5–30 cm) Flowers: mid May–end June

Lewisia is one of the most colourful rockery plants — bright flowers with petals which are often striped. Unfortunately, leafy rosettes may rot in winter if not protected. Grow one of the L. cotyledon hybrids.

Lewisia cotyledon

MAZUS Mazus — *Deciduous*
Ht: 2 in. (5 cm) Flowers: mid June–early Aug

A ground-hugging plant related to Mimulus. It has never become popular although the purple flowers of M. reptans are quite unusual — two-lipped and marked with white and yellow. 'Albus' is a white variety.

MORISIA Morisia — *Deciduous*
Ht: 1 in. (2.5 cm) Flowers: end March–mid May

M. monanthos forms a neat and compact cushion of dark and shiny leaves. It flowers early — the 4-petalled blooms are stalkless. Both full sun and a gritty planting mixture are essential.

Mazus reptans

Deciduous: Stems/leaves die in winter   *Evergreen: Stems/leaves retained over winter*

Primula 'Wanda'

Ramonda myconi

Rhodohypoxis baurii

Sempervivum arachnoideum

PHLOX Dwarf Phlox
Deciduous

Ht: *4-6 in. (10-15 cm)* ***Flowers:*** *mid May-end June*

An excellent plant for the raised bed or alpine trough — it will cover rocks or trail over the sides, bearing masses of ½ in. blooms in late spring and early summer. Grow a variety of P. subulata or P. douglasii.

PRIMULA Rockery Primrose
Evergreen or Deciduous

Ht: *2-6 in. (5-15 cm)* ***Flowers:*** *mid March-mid May*

There are many species and varieties of Primula which are dwarf enough for container growing — see The Rock & Water Garden Expert for examples. The basic pattern is a basal leafy rosette with flowers on stalks.

RAMONDA Ramonda
Evergreen

Ht: *4-6 in. (10-15 cm)* ***Flowers:*** *mid April-mid May*

Ramonda is included here as an example of an alpine which flourishes in shady conditions. The one to grow is R. myconi — the flowers are large with a golden centre. Protect the leaves from winter rain.

RAOULIA Scabweed
Evergreen

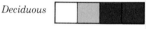

Ht: *½ in. (1 cm)* ***Flowers:*** *end April-early June*

You can't mistake this one — the tiny leaves form a silvery mat over the soil surface which changes to yellow as the minute flowers open. Grow R. australis, tenuicaulis or lutescens — protect from winter rain.

RHODOHYPOXIS Rhodohypoxis
Deciduous

Ht: *2 in. (5 cm)* ***Flowers:*** *end April-early Sept*

Not as easy or reliable as many of the plants in this list, but its exceptionally long flowering season makes it worth trying in a sheltered spot. Choose a variety of R. baurii — the stalked flowers have 6 petals.

SAXIFRAGA Saxifrage
Evergreen

Ht: *2-12 in. (5-30 cm)* ***Flowers:*** *mid May-mid July*

One of the basic rockery perennials — many species and varieties are available. Leafy mats or cushions produce upright flower stalks which bear loose clusters of starry blooms. See The Rock & Water Garden Expert.

SEDUM Stonecrop
Evergreen

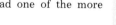

Ht: *2-4 in. (5-10 cm)* ***Flowers:*** *mid June-end July*

A very popular and easy rock garden plant — starry flowers arise from a mat of fleshy leaves. Avoid the invasive S. acre — grow instead one of the more attractive and compact varieties with coloured foliage.

SEMPERVIVUM Houseleek
Evergreen

Ht: *3-6 in. (7.5-15 cm)* ***Flowers:*** *mid July-early Sept*

The leaves are fleshy and are grouped into rosettes. Offsets are produced — the mother rosette dies after flowering. The flower stalks are thick and bear multi-petalled blooms. Various leaf colours are available.

VIOLA Rockery Violet
Deciduous

Ht: *4-8 in. (10-20 cm)* ***Flowers:*** *depends on type*

Violas and Pansies are best known as bedding plants, but there are numerous dwarf perennials. Examples include V. biflora (yellow), V. jooi (lavender), V. gracilis (various) and V. lutea (yellow).

Deciduous: Stems/leaves die in winter   *Evergreen: Stems/leaves retained over winter*

PLANT TYPE:
BULBS

Spring-flowering bulbs are one of the mainstays of container gardening. The open garden can rely on flowering shrubs and massed plantings of biennials to provide bright March and April colour. For the pot and the trough we rely on Tulips, Daffodils and Crocuses to serve as the main heralds of spring.

It is not necessary to wait until spring for a display of bulbs in containers. You can have a January–February display — Snowdrop, Winter Aconite, Iris reticulata, Cyclamen coum, Chionodoxa and Anemone blanda are examples. Spring is, of course, the major display season and you should try a few of the more unusual ones listed on the following pages as well as the universal favourites such as Hyacinth, Tulip and so on.

Spring should not be the end of the container bulb year. Summer pots can be brightened up with Gladiolus, Lily, tuberous Begonia etc and for autumn and winter flowers you can plant Nerine, autumn-flowering Crocus and Cyclamen.

With careful planning and several containers you can have bulbs in flower nearly all year round. Small and choice varieties which may be almost invisible in the open garden become things of beauty when brought closer to eye level. In addition many bulbs do better in containers than in the open garden because they are grown in an ideal medium with adequate drainage. All this sounds as if bulbs are ideal container plants, but in fact they suffer from three drawbacks.

Firstly, the flowering period is often quite short compared with the average bedding plant. Secondly, there are the non-decorative periods when the bulb is dormant before starting into growth and then there are the dead and dying leaves after flowering. Finally, specimens in containers rarely put on enough leaf growth to produce worthwhile bulbs for a second year's display. Because of these drawbacks it is worth considering the various ways of using bulbs in containers — some of them are designed to overcome one or more of the drawbacks:

- SINGLE-TYPE PLANTING This method simply ignores the drawbacks. Bulbs are planted up and the floral display is enjoyed, after which they are lifted for later planting in the garden.

- LAYER PLANTING Two or more types of bulbs with different flowering seasons are planted in layers so as to extend the display time.

- IN-POT PLANTING The bulbs are grown in pots and when the buds are beginning to open are then set out in the container. After flowering the pots are removed and replaced by other plants.

- PART PLANTING This method relies on the presence of other plants in the container to disguise the pre-flowering and the dying-down stages.

Filling & Planting

STEP 2:
FINISH PLANTING
Sift compost between the bulbs and then add more of the planting medium so that a 1–2 in. (2.5–5 cm) watering space is left at the top of the container. There are two alternative techniques. In layer planting the addition of this compost stops at an earlier stage so that a layer of smaller bulbs can be added (for example Crocuses over Daffodils) in order to extend the display. Another variant is part planting — here the trees, shrubs and/or bedding plants are put in first and the bulbs are then planted with a trowel to the correct depth in the compost. Whichever technique you use the compost should be kept moist and the bulbs should be lifted when the display is over for later planting in the garden

STEP 1:
BEGIN PLANTING
Prepare the container, put it in place and add the drainage and optional peat layer as shown on page 16. Now add soilless potting compost, pressing down gently with your hands. Stop adding compost when the correct height is reached — which is when the bulbs placed on the layer will be covered with the recommended height of compost, measured from the tip of the bulb to the top of the growing medium. Buy bulbs which are large, firm and healthy — place them on the compost with little space (approximately 1 in.) between them

Anemone blanda

Begonia pendula

Colchicum speciosum 'Album'

Eranthis hyemalis

ANEMONE Windflower   *Planting depth: 2 in.*
Ht: 6–9 in. (15–22.5 cm) **Flowers:** *depends on type*

Two types — Daisy-flowered ones such as A. blanda (plant in September for February flowers) and Poppy-flowered ones like the Brigid strain (plant in November for April flowers or in April for October flowers).

BEGONIA Tuberous Begonia *Planting depth: tip above surface*
Ht: 6–18 in. (15–45 cm) **Flowers:** *mid June–end Sept*

Plant the tubers under glass in March or April — set out in June. Several types available — the large-flowered B. tuberhybrida, the smaller but more floriferous B. multiflora and the trailing B. pendula.

CHIONODOXA Glory of the Snow   *Planting depth: 3 in.*
Ht: 4–8 in. (10–20 cm) **Flowers:** *mid Feb–mid March*

The 6-petalled starry flowers are borne in dainty sprays. Blue is the usual colour but other shades are available. Plant in September. C. luciliae is the popular one — C. gigantea has the largest flowers.

COLCHICUM Autumn Crocus   *Planting depth: 3 in.*
Ht: 6 in. (15 cm) **Flowers:** *mid Sept–early Nov*

It looks like a Crocus but is not related. The goblet-shaped blooms rise up through the compost in autumn before the leaves appear. Netted and striped varieties are available. Plant in August — take care, Colchicum is poisonous.

CROCOSMIA Montbretia   *Planting depth: 3 in.*
Ht: 18–24 in. (45–60 cm) **Flowers:** *end July–early Sept*

A showy plant for a large container. Trumpet-shaped flowers are borne on upright or arching wiry stems above the sword-like leaves. A sunny, sheltered spot is necessary. Plant in March.

CROCUS Crocus   *Planting depth: 3 in.*
Ht: 3–5 in. (7.5–12.5 cm) **Flowers:** *depends on type*

The yellow and blue wineglass-shaped flowers of the spring-flowering hybrids are a familiar sight in March and April but there are also winter- and autumn-flowering species — see The Flower Expert or Bulb Expert for details.

CYCLAMEN Cyclamen   *Planting depth: 1 in.*
Ht: 3–6 in. (7.5–15 cm) **Flowers:** *depends on type*

Although better known as a house plant, there are several hardy species with 1 in. flowers with swept-back petals which can be grown outdoors. There are winter-, spring-, summer- and autumn-flowering types.

ERANTHIS Winter Aconite   *Planting depth: 2 in.*
Ht: 3–4 in. (7.5–10 cm) **Flowers:** *end Jan–mid March*

Plant with Snowdrops in September and they will bloom at the same time — yellow flowers with a collar of deeply-divided leaves. E. tubergenii is a large-flowered hybrid.

ERYTHRONIUM Dog's-tooth Violet   *Planting depth: 3 in.*
Ht: 6 in. (15 cm) **Flowers:** *end March–end April*

E. dens-canis bears nodding star-shaped flowers above leaves which are mottled with brown markings. Plant in September or October in a partially shaded spot. There are a few species which grow 12 in. (30 cm) high.

FRITILLARIA Fritillary　　　　*Planting depth: 4 in.*
Ht: *12 in. (30 cm)* **Flowers:** *end March–end April*
Choose one of the varieties of the Snake's Head Fritillary (F. meleagris) with chequered-patterned petals. In spring the bell-like flowers hang down from the top of the upright stems. The planting time is September–October.

Fritillaria meleagris

GALANTHUS Snowdrop　　　　*Planting depth: 4 in.*
Ht: *5 in. (12.5 cm)* **Flowers:** *end Jan–mid March*
In many gardens the nodding white blooms of Snowdrops are the first garden flowers of the year. The Common Snowdrop (G. nivalis) bears single flowers — the variety 'Flore Pleno' has double globular blooms. Plant in September.

GLADIOLUS Sword Lily　　　　*Planting depth: 4 in.*
Ht: *12–24 in. (30–60 cm)* **Flowers:** *depends on type*
Not all the groups of this popular garden flower are suitable as container plants. Choose one of the Miniature Hybrids (plant in April for August flowers) or a Species variety (plant in October for May flowers).

HYACINTHUS Hyacinth　　　　*Planting depth: 6 in.*
Ht: *6–12 in. (15–30 cm)* **Flowers:** *early March–end April*
Hyacinths provide colour and fragrance. Plant in September. The Dutch Hyacinths have tightly-packed flower-heads in many colours — the Roman Hyacinths have loose flower-heads in white, pink or purple.

Ipheion uniflorum

IPHEION Spring Starflower　　　　*Planting depth: 2 in.*
Ht: *6 in. (15 cm)* **Flowers:** *mid April–mid May*
An easy but unusual bulb which is worth trying. Fragrant starry blooms appear singly on the top of each flower stalk. Plant in September–October. Listed as Ipheion, Brodiaea, Milla or Triteleia.

IRIS Iris　　　　*Planting depth: 2 in.*
Ht: *4–6 in. (10–15 cm)* **Flowers:** *mid Jan–mid March*
There are many bulbous Irises — the favourite container ones belong to the Reticulata group. Included are I. danfordiae (yellow), I. reticulata (purple) and I. histrioides 'Major' (blue). Plant in September.

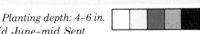

Iris danfordiae

LEUCOJUM Snowflake　　　　*Planting depth: 4 in.*
Ht: *8 in. (20 cm)* **Flowers:** *mid Feb–mid March*
The Spring Snowflake (L. vernum) bears ¾ in. wide bells on upright stalks — it is easy to confuse it with a tall-growing Snowdrop. Plant as soon as bulbs are available in August.

LILIUM Lily　　　　*Planting depth: 4–6 in.*
Ht: *12–48 in. (30–120 cm)* **Flowers:** *mid June–mid Sept*
Many types can be grown in containers — L. auratum, longiflorum, hansonii, regale, martagon etc. Look for the dwarf (12–18 in.) hybrids. Lilies are best grown in a pot on their own. Plant out bulbs as soon as possible after buying.

MUSCARI Grape Hyacinth　　　　*Planting depth: 3 in.*
Ht: *6–9 in. (15–22.5 cm)* **Flowers:** *early April–early May*
Each fleshy flower stalk bears a mass of tiny, bell-like blooms. Clumps of Grape Hyacinth are often planted beneath conifers or between showier plants in mixed displays. Plant in September.

Muscari armeniacum

Puschkinia scilloides

Sisyrinchium bellum

Sternbergia lutea

Tigridia pavonia

NARCISSUS Daffodil   *Planting depth: twice bulb height*
Ht: 4–12 in. (10–30 cm) **Flowers:** *end Feb–end April*

There are hundreds of Narcissi varieties, but for containers it is best to choose from the Dwarf and Cyclamineus groups. Included here are N. 'Minnow', triandrus albus, 'Tête-à-Tête' and bulbocodium. Plant in August.

NERINE Nerine   *Planting depth: 4 in.*
Ht: 24 in. (60 cm) **Flowers:** *mid Sept–mid Oct*

Nerines are better known as indoor plants but there is a hardy species (N. bowdenii) which can be grown in a large container. A cluster of spidery-petalled flowers are borne on tall stalks. Plant in April.

PUSCHKINIA Striped Squill   *Planting depth: 2 in.*
Ht: 4 in. (10 cm) **Flowers:** *mid March–mid April*

This relative of the Bluebell has never been popular, which is surprising. The open starry bells of P. scilloides are pale blue with a dark blue stripe. A white variety is available. Plant in September.

SCHIZOSTYLIS Kaffir Lily   *Planting depth: ½ in.*
Ht: 24 in. (60 cm) **Flowers:** *mid Sept–end Oct*

This is one for a large container and a gardener who likes a challenge. The flower stalks of S. coccinea bear clusters of bright red starry blooms with waxy petals. The variety 'Mrs Hegarty' is pink. Plant in April.

SCILLA Bluebell   *Planting depth: 4 in.*
Ht: 3–12 in. (7.5–30 cm) **Flowers:** *depends on type*

The 9 in. tall English Bluebell with blue drooping flowers in April is well-known, but there are many others blooming between February and June with bell-like or starry flowers — see The Flower Expert. Plant in August–September.

SISYRINCHIUM Sisyrinchium   *Planting depth: ½ in.*
Ht: 4 in. (10 cm) **Flowers:** *mid May–early Sept*

The smaller Sisyrinchiums are useful for growing between taller and showier plants — the flowering season is exceptionally long. Grow S. bellum (mauve) or S. brachypus (yellow). Plant in April.

STERNBERGIA Yellow Star Flower   *Planting depth: 5 in.*
Ht: 6 in. (15 cm) **Flowers:** *mid Sept–mid Oct*

Apart from the presence of a distinct flower stalk the bloom looks very similar to a yellow late-flowering Crocus. A good plant for an alpine trough — full sun is essential. Plant in August–September.

TIGRIDIA Tiger Flower   *Planting depth: 4 in.*
Ht: 18 in. (45 cm) **Flowers:** *end July–mid Sept*

A showy beauty for the end of summer which is grown in very few gardens. The inner petals of the open 4 in. wide flowers are splashed with red and purple. T. pavonia is the only species. Plant in April.

TULIPA Tulip   *Planting depth: 6 in.*
Ht: 6–12 in. (15–30 cm) **Flowers:** *mid March–early May*

For the garden bed and border there is a bewildering array from which to choose. For containers it is best to choose from the low-growing Species group — T. kaufmanniana, fosteriana, greigii, praestans etc. Plant in November.

The display of spring bulbs in a container need not always be a riot of colour. Here a small cluster of Snowdrops in a terracotta wall pot announce that winter is coming to an end — the display is greatly helped by the Ivy backcloth ▷

◁ A classical spring arrangement, as illustrated on page 42. Tulipa 'Apricot Beauty' are the dot plants, Hyacinthus 'King of the Blues' are the filler plants, Universal Pansies are the edging plants and Ivies are the trailers

△ A massed spring arrangement in which bulbs are dominant. Within the terracotta window box the Tulips, Daffodils, Hyacinths and Grape Hyacinths blend happily with the Forget-me-nots, Polyanthus, Pansies and Ivies

PLANT TYPE:
ROSES

Growing Roses in tubs on the patio is a welcome addition to the plants in the beds and borders of the garden, but for the apartment owner the container on the balcony is the *only* way to grow Roses. The first step is to choose the right container — some experts believe that the half-barrel is the only truly satisfactory home, but suitable pots, tubs and urns in a variety of materials are available. Size is more important than material. A good root run is essential, which means a minimum depth of 12 in. (30 cm) for Miniature and compact Patio Roses and 18 in. (45 cm) for all other types.

Prepare the container in the usual way (see page 16) for the Rose you have bought. Use a soil-based compost such as John Innes No.3. Plant between spring and autumn if it is container-grown or in either October–November or March if it is a bare-root specimen. Generally it is better to buy a container-grown specimen from a garden centre rather than sending off for a bare-root one — you can see just what you are getting if you wait until it is in flower before making your purchase.

When making your choice you will be confronted by a large selection of many types at the garden centre or in the catalogue. Take care — not all are suitable for containers. Roses are sometimes grown in tubs at the base of the house wall to provide a climbing display. Do not use a Rambler for this purpose — choose instead one of the modern large-flowered Climbers such as 'Aloha', 'Compassion', 'Golden Showers' or 'Swan Lake'. Hybrid Teas and Floribundas will grow, but not as well as in the garden — avoid all types described as tall and upright. Standards can be grown if proper staking is provided. There are just two groups, however, which are really at home in the container — the Patio and the Miniature Rose. In addition you can grow one of the County series of Ground-cover Roses ('Hertfordshire', 'Suffolk' etc) if you want a wide-spreading specimen.

The Patio Rose is a dwarf cluster-flowered variety which grows 18–24 in. (45–60 cm) high. The Miniature Rose is even more compact, with a maximum height of 15 in. (37.5 cm). When making your choice colour and flower form will be the main considerations, but do check the growth habit — most are bushy but some are upright and others are wide-spreading.

Edging the container with spring-flowering subjects such as Polyanthus and miniature bulbs or planting with trailers such as Lobelia is a matter of personal taste. The cultural rules, however, must be followed. Place the container in a sunny spot away from overhanging trees. Water during dry weather but never keep the compost permanently wet.

Feed twice a year with a rose fertilizer — water the compost before using a powder or granulated fertilizer and rake in lightly afterwards.

Rosa 'Angela Rippon'

Rosa 'Sweet Dream'

Rosa 'Top Marks'

RECOMMENDED ROSES

VARIETY	TYPE	DESCRIPTION
ANGELA RIPPON	M	The double blooms are rosy salmon pink, freely borne amongst the healthy foliage. Bushy growth, slightly fragrant.
ANNA FORD	P	Each orange-red flower is yellow at the base — the bushy growth bears masses of these small semi-double blooms.
CIDER CUP	P	The trusses bear many double, dark apricot blooms — both flowers and leaves are small. Growth is bushy.
CLARISSA	P	Apricot-coloured blooms appear in large clusters on tall and upright plants. Flowers are double Hybrid Tea type.
CONSERVATION	P	Bushy growth habit — the double flowers are apricot pink. Scent is slight and leaves are small.
DARLING FLAME	M	Healthy upright plant — the double blooms are orange-red with a golden reverse. Grows about 12 in. (30 cm) high.
EASTER MORNING	M	Ivory white double blooms are set among small shiny leaves. Healthy, but not a profuse bloomer.
FLOWER CARPET	P	Choose this one for spreading growth. The double flowers are deep pink. Glossy leaves, healthy growth.
GENTLE TOUCH	P	Pale pink — blooms have a lovely Hybrid Tea shape when young. Flower trusses are large and sturdy. Highly recommended.
GINGERNUT	P	Bushy growth with small glossy leaves. Flowers are double with bronze-orange petals and a darker reverse.
GOLDEN SUNBLAZE	M	An upright plant — probably the best yellow Miniature. The blooms have a Hybrid Tea shape. Also called 'Rise 'n' Shine'.
HAKUUN	P	A healthy prolific bloomer — the trusses bear many creamy white flowers which are small and semi-double.
MAGIC CARROUSEL	M	Unusual — each double flower has creamy petals with distinct crimson edges. Grows about 15 in. (37.5 cm) high.
PEEK-A-BOO	P	One of the earliest of the modern Patio Roses, and still one of the best for containers. Flowers apricot to pink.
PRETTY POLLY	P	A good tub plant with dense and rounded growth. It blooms profusely, producing clusters of pink double blooms.
QUEEN MOTHER	P	A spreading plant which grows about 18 in. (45 cm) high. The semi-double pink flowers open wide when mature.
RED ACE	M	A highly recommended Miniature. The semi-double blooms are dark red and velvety. Growth is upright.
REGENSBERG	P	One of the so-called 'painted' varieties — large, flat blooms of white splashed with pink. Bushy growth.
STARINA	M	Still one of the stars of the Miniature world — well-formed orange-red flowers all season long. Upright growth.
SWEET DREAM	P	Very popular and much praised. Growth is dense and cushion-like — peachy blooms are well-formed.
SWEET MAGIC	P	The deep orange petals fade to golden yellow with age, giving a glowing effect. Fragrance is quite pronounced.
TOP MARKS	P	Few Roses can match the free-flowering nature of this variety — large clusters of bright orange-red flowers are borne in profusion.
TRUMPETER	P	A bright and showy variety — the trusses bear masses of orange-red flowers all season long. Good disease resistance.

M: Miniature Rose   **P: Patio Rose**

PLANT TYPE:
AQUATIC PLANTS

Water in the garden has a special attraction which is hard to explain — it is a focal point which hardly any other feature can match. If you are lucky enough to have a pond then stocking it with plants and fish is an important but somewhat tricky task. A proper choice of plants is essential if you are to create the right balance which will ensure clear water.

By the definition on page 3 a well-stocked garden pond is a container — 'a receptacle for growing plants which is not fully open to the garden soil below'. There are two advantages of the pond as a home for plants — they do not require watering and the aquatic types are less often seen and therefore attract more attention than the usual run of garden plants.

Of course we do not regard the ordinary garden pond as a container, but there is a container for housing individual aquatic plants which has become increasingly popular — the aquatic basket decribed on page 20. The traditional way to plant has been to set the roots in a layer of soil at the bottom of the pond. The drawbacks include the stirring up of mud by fish, the unwanted spread of invasive species and the difficulty of lifting up plants for dividing and replanting every few years. All of these difficulties are avoided by using aquatic baskets.

You don't have to build a pond to enjoy aquatic plants — a minipond is a water-holding container which is stood or built on a patio or balcony and houses one or more aquatic plants. There are several reasons for choosing a minipond rather than a regular-sized one. Shortage of space is the usual reason, but the elimination of the need for large scale excavation is often an equally important consideration. In addition the plants are brought closer to eye level and the chore of routine maintenance is reduced. Finally there is the undesirability of having a large stretch of water where active and unsupervised toddlers are present — care, however, is still necessary.

The minipond can be made from bricks or blocks with a waterproof lining — this may be a rigid fibreglass liner, flexible butyl sheeting or pond paint. It is more usual to use a ready-made waterproof container such as a bitumen-coated half-barrel, sink, fibreglass tank or large plastic trough.

Two basic types of plant are grown in a half-barrel minipond. The Deep-water aquatics have submerged roots, leaves on the surface and flowers on or above the surface. Water Lilies can be included here, but only the most compact dwarfs can be used. The Marginals are generally planted closer to the surface — they have submerged roots but the leaves and flowers are clearly above the surface. A Goldfish or two can be kept in the minipond if it is at least 15 in. (37.5 cm) deep, but in a thin-walled small container fish will not be happy as water temperatures will fluctuate widely during the year.

Planting a Pond

STEP 1:
LINE THE BASKET

Use hessian — Finofil and louvred baskets do not need lining

STEP 2:
FILL THE BASKET

Use heavy loam from which twigs, roots etc have been removed. Do not add peat or compost — enrich with a little Bone Meal

STEP 4:
ADD GRIT LAYER

Place a 1 in. (2.5 cm) layer of pea shingle on top of the soil to prevent soil disturbance by fish

STEP 3:
PLANT UP THE BASKET

The correct time is between May and September — not in the dormant season. Firm planting is essential

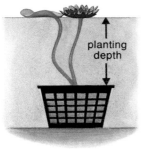

planting depth

STEP 5:
PUT THE BASKET IN THE POND

Water thoroughly. Deep-water aquatics should be introduced to the pond gradually. Stand the basket on a brick or two so that the crown is about 2 in. (5 cm) below the surface. Remove bricks as plants start to grow

Planting a Minipond

STEP 2:
PREPARE THE CONTAINER

Varnish the outside of a half-barrel and treat the inside with a bitumen paint. Place it in a sunny or partially sunny spot and away from trees if fish are to be introduced. Partially fill with water

STEP 1:
CHOOSE THE CONTAINER

The minipond must be weatherproof, water-proof, non-corrosive and non-toxic. It should be at least 18 in. (45 cm) across and hold at least 5 gallons (23 litres) of water

STEP 3:
PLANT ONE OR MORE DEEP-WATER AQUATICS

Set the Deep-water aquatic plants in the water as instructed above. Support the basket on bricks until new leaves have started to grow if the recommended planting depth is more than 6 in. (15 cm)

STEP 4:
PLANT ONE OR MORE MARGINALS

There are a number of Marginals to choose from — a selection appears on page 82 and a more complete list in The Rock & Water Garden Expert. Mark a line on the inside of the container 2 in. (5 cm) below the top — this will be the water level when the minipond is finished. Set the basket so that the height from the crown to the line is the recommended planting depth

STEP 5:
ADD MORE WATER

When planting is finished add more water until the water level line is reached. Wait a month before introducing Goldfish

AQUATIC PLANTS FOR THE MINIPOND

Aponogeton distachyos

Eichhornia crassipes

Iris laevigata

Nymphaea pygmaea 'Helvola'

APONOGETON Water Hawthorn   *Deep-water aquatic*

Ht: Floating ***Flowers:*** *spring and autumn*

The floral spikes float on the surface — each flower has white petals and black anthers. An easy plant which flowers for months — the blotched oblong leaves are evergreen. Planting depth 12 in. (30 cm).

CALTHA Marsh Marigold   *Marginal*

Ht: 9 in. (22.5 cm) ***Flowers:*** *April*

The best one to grow where space is limited is C. palustris 'Plena' — the heart-shaped leaves form compact mounds about 9 in. (22.5 cm) across and the double yellow flowers cover the foliage. Planting depth 1 in. (2.5 cm).

EICHHORNIA Water Hyacinth   *Floater*

Ht: 9 in. (22.5 cm) ***Flowers:*** *July–Sept*

Something different — a floating plant which you drop on the surface. The Orchid-like lavender blue flowers are borne on spikes. Lift the plant in September. Keep indoors in a bowl of muddy water — replace in June.

IRIS Japanese Water Iris   *Marginal*

Ht: 18 in. (45 cm) ***Flowers:*** *June*

I. laevigata is a popular pond plant — the 5 in. (12.5 cm) wide blooms are blue with a yellow central stripe. White, rose-pink and blue-blotched varieties are available. Planting depth 1–2 in. (2.5–5 cm).

MENYANTHES Bog Bean   *Marginal*

Ht: 9 in. (22.5 cm) ***Flowers:*** *May–June*

The starry flowers are borne on upright spikes — the pink buds open into white blooms with petals fringed at the edges. Leaves are made up of 3 leaflets. Planting depth 1–3 in. (2.5–7.5 cm).

MYRIOPHYLLUM Parrot's Feather   *Marginal*

Ht: 6 in. (15 cm) ***Foliage:*** *June–Nov*

M. proserpinacoides has feathery leaves on sprawling stems which float and also rise above the surface. The exposed shoots are killed by frost in winter — the crown below the ice will survive. Planting depth 5 in. (12.5 cm).

NYMPHAEA Dwarf Water Lily   *Deep-water aquatic*

Ht: 0–2 in. (0–5 cm) ***Flowers:*** *June–Sept*

Choose one of the dwarfs recommended in The Rock & Water Garden Expert. Examples include N. pygmaea 'Helvola' (pale yellow), N. candida (white) and N. 'Aurora' (deep orange). Planting depth 4–8 in. (10–20 cm).

PONTEDERIA Pickerel Weed   *Marginal*

Ht: 24 in. (60 cm) ***Flowers:*** *July–Sept*

In summer the flower stalks arise among the large oval leaves. The tops of the stalks are clothed with masses of small, funnel-shaped blue blooms. Divide the clumps every few years. Planting depth 4–5 in. (10–12.5 cm).

TYPHA Reedmace   *Marginal*

Ht: 12–18 in. (30–45 cm) ***Flowers:*** *June–July*

You can grow a 'Bulrush' if you choose the dwarf T. minima. The dense brown flower-heads are oval (1½ in. long) and are borne on slender stalks above the grass-like leaves. Planting depth 2–5 in. (5–12.5 cm).

Ht: Height above water

PLANT TYPE:
VEGETABLES

It is obvious that virtually any vegetable can be grown in a container provided that the receptacle is large enough, the compost is suitable and the requirements for water, fertilizer, support and so on are catered for. This does not mean, however, that it is necessarily a good idea to use some of your containers for this purpose — the experts cannot agree among themselves.

Some gardening advisers stress the advantages of growing crops in pots, troughs, or growing bags. Fewer soil pest headaches, no heavy clay problems, no digging and weeding... as a result a wide range of vegetables are recommended for growing on the patio. Other experts feel that the amount of food you can grow by this method is strictly limited and the plants are usually either non-decorative or downright ugly. Accordingly, they consider that vegetables are not worth the chore of regular watering and so containers are recommended only for decorative flowers, bulbs, shrubs and trees.

A middle course is proposed here. Not even the most avid supporter of container vegetables would recommend really bulky plants such as Brussels Sprouts, Kale, Broccoli etc for pots or growing bags. Many other types of crop can be grown, but there would seem to be no point in growing 'ordinary' vegetables if space is available for them in the open garden. However, there are several situations where vegetables are worth their place in containers.

Firstly, there are the vegetables which are decorative in their own right. A Tomato plant with a long line of Cherry-sized fruits, a group of Runner Beans with colourful flowers, a Ruby Chard plant with bright red stalks and leaf veins, the feathery leaves of Carrots and the red-veined leaves of Beetroot can be a welcome decorative addition to some part planting schemes among the bedding plants.

Next, a number of rather tender vegetables can suffer in the open garden in some districts but may flourish in the shelter and warmth of a south-facing wall — examples here are Aubergine, Cucumber, Capsicum and Tomato. Finally, there are the neat salad crops which can be crowded into growing bags and provide fresh vegetables without having to walk to the vegetable plot — Radish, Onion, Lettuce etc.

So there are a number of virtues in growing some vegetables in containers, but in nearly all gardens they play only a minor or non-existent role. The situation is different for people who do not have a garden — those who rely on a balcony, rooftop or courtyard garden sometimes devote most of their containers to the production of home-grown vegetables.

Any pot, tub or trough which is deeper than 8 in. (20 cm) can be used, but the favourite container these days is the growing bag — see page 35.

ALL-OVER PLANTING

Most vegetables are grown on their own in a container — the Aubergine in its pot, the Tomato and Courgette in their growing bags and so on. 'All-over' means growing one variety and not usually just one specimen — several Runner Bean, Lettuce and Radish plants have to be grown to make the crop worthwhile.

PART PLANTING

A number of vegetables are often recommended for planting among bedding plants or as part of a mixed scheme of perennials, bulbs and annuals. Popular ones for part planting include Carrot, Radish, Spring Onion, Beetroot and Loose-leaf Lettuce. This approach is more often seen in textbooks than in the garden.

Aubergine 'Black Prince'

Courgette 'Gold Rush'

Cucumber 'Amslic'

French Bean 'The Prince'

AUBERGINE

The Aubergine or Egg Plant is rather tender outdoors, like Tomato. Raise seedlings under glass — sow seed in a compost-filled pot in March. Harden off and plant out at the end of May — one in a 10 in. (25 cm) pot or 3 in a growing bag. If possible cover seedlings with a cloche. Remove the growing point when the plant is 12 in. (30 cm) high — stake stems. Remove lateral shoots and remaining flowers when 5 fruits have formed. Cut each fruit when about 6 in. (15 cm) long. Varieties: **'Moneymaker'**, **'Black Prince'**, **'Bonica'**.

BEETROOT

Globe varieties of Beetroot grow well in pots, troughs and growing bags. Sow seed 1 in. deep in mid April–late May — thin the seedlings to leave plants 4 in. (10 cm) apart. Avoid any check to growth — harvest when no larger than a tennis ball. Varieties: **'Boltardy'**, **'Monopoly'**, **'Monodet'**.

CAPSICUM

Sweet Pepper is rather tender outdoors, like Tomato. Raise seedlings under glass — sow seed in a compost-filled pot in March. Harden off and plant out in early June — one in a 10 in. (25 cm) pot or 3 in a growing bag. If possible cover seedlings with a cloche. Pick at the green or orange stage when fruits are swollen and glossy. Varieties: **'Canape'**, **'New Ace'**, **'Gypsy'**, **'Ariane'**.

CARROT

A suitable crop for growing bags or for mixed plantings in pots and troughs. Choose one of the short-rooted varieties which are golf ball round or finger long. Sow seed ½ in. deep in end March–end April for a July crop. Thin out seedlings when large enough to handle to leave plants 2–3 in. (5–7.5 cm) apart. Pull up small Carrots as required. Varieties: **'Early French Frame'**, **'Amsterdam Forcing'**.

COURGETTE

A good vegetable for a growing bag — the bushy or sprawling stems and large leaves soon cover the bag and the summer flowers are followed by green or yellow fruits. Sow seed 1 in. deep in late May or early June in the container where they are to grow — one in a tub or 2 in a growing bag. Keep the compost moist at all times — water around the plants, not over them. Cut the fruits when they are still quite small (4 in. long) — continual cropping is essential to prolong the fruiting period. Varieties: **'Zucchini'**, **'Gold Rush'**, **'Green Bush'**.

CUCUMBER

Once the outdoor or ridge Cucumber was always short and dumpy with bumps and warts, but not any more. There are now varieties with smooth skins and excellent flavour which look like greenhouse ones. Cucumbers can be grown in a raised bed, tub or growing bag — choose a sunny spot. Sow 3 seeds 1 in. deep and a few inches apart at the centre of the container or in a growing bag planting pocket in late May–early June. Thin out to leave the strongest seedling. Pinch out the growing tip when the plant has developed 6 or 7 leaves. Side-shoots will then develop and these can be left to trail or be trained up netting or stakes. Keep the soil moist — water around the plants, not over them. Use a sharp knife to remove the fruits when they are about 8 in. (20 cm) long. Varieties: **'Burpless Tasty Green'**, **'Long Green Ridge'**, **'Amslic'**.

FRENCH BEAN

The standard varieties are bushy plants with white, pink or red flowers followed by 4–6 in. (10–15 cm) long pods. There are variations — you can buy purple- and yellow-podded types as well as climbing ones. A standard growing bag will support 8–12 plants — sow seeds 2 in. deep in early June. Provide the stems with short twigs for support — climbing varieties will grow about 5 ft (150 cm) high and will need more robust support. Begin picking when the pods are about 4 in. long. Varieties: **'Masterpiece'**, **'The Prince'**, **'Kinghorn Wax'** (yellow), **'Purple-podded Climbing'** (purple, climbing).

LETTUCE

It is perhaps best to confine the large-headed varieties to the vegetable plot. There are two types which are at home in containers — the miniatures which produce tennis ball sized heads and the loose-leaf varieties with frilly and often red or bronzy leaves which are decorative enough for mixed plantings with bedding plants. These loose-leaf varieties have little or no heart so a few leaves can be removed on a cut-and-come-again basis. Sow seed ½ in. deep in April–May — thin the seedlings as soon as the first leaves appear in order to avoid overcrowding. A growing bag will support about 12 plants. Varieties: **'Little Gem'**, **'Tom Thumb'** (miniature), **'Salad Bowl'**, **'Red Salad Bowl'**, **'Lollo Rossa'**, **'Rossimo'** (loose-leaf).

Lettuce 'Little Gem'

ONION

Salad (Spring) Onions are the ones to grow — white-skinned, mild-flavoured varieties which are picked when the bulbs are still small. Sow seeds thinly ½ in. deep in 4 in. (10 cm) wide rows in a growing bag. The time to sow is March–July for a June–October crop or in August for Onions in March–May. Thin the seedlings to leave 1 in. (2.5 cm) spacings — harvest when the bulbs are about ¾ in. (2 cm) across. Variety: **'White Lisbon'**.

PEA

'Ordinary' peas are not really a good container crop — yields are quite small for the area occupied and results are often disappointing. If you do want to grow your own pods for shelling then choose a dwarf early variety. It is a better idea to try instead the novelty Winged Pea — a bushy plant which bears red flowers which are followed by curiously shaped winged pods. These are cooked whole like Mangetout. A standard growing bag will support about 8 plants — sow seeds 1 in. deep in late May. Provide the stems with short twigs for support. Gather the pods when they are 1–2 in. long — they become fibrous and stringy if left to mature. Varieties: **'Hurst Beagle'**, **'Feltham First'** (ordinary), **'Asparagus Pea'** (winged).

Spring Onion 'White Lisbon'

POTATO

Buy a potato barrel (see page 20) if you want to grow Potatoes — some models have slide-up panels at the base to enable you to check the state of the crop and to harvest a few tubers at a time. Prepare the seed Potatoes by standing them eyes uppermost in trays in a light frost-free room. In 4–6 weeks there will be several 1 in. (2.5 cm) shoots — the Potatoes are ready for planting. Place a 4 in. (10 cm) layer of compost in the barrel — stand 4 sprouted Potatoes on top and cover them with a 6 in. layer of compost. When the shoots are 6 in. high cover with more compost until only the tips are showing. Repeat the process until the top of the barrel is nearly reached. There is little point in growing a maincrop variety — choose instead a first early and plant in either late March for a July crop or plant in July (cover stems on a frosty night) for a Christmas crop. Varieties: **'Arran Pilot'**, **'Duke of York'**.

Asparagus Pea

RADISH

A quick-maturing salad crop which can be used to fill bare spots between other food plants in containers or on their own in growing bags where they are sown in 3 rows. Sow the seed about ½ in. deep and thin so that the seedlings are 1–2 in. (2.5–5 cm) apart. Make repeat sowings from mid-spring to midsummer. Harvest while the Radishes are still young — overgrown specimens are woody and hollow. Varieties: **'Cherry Belle'**, **'Scarlet Globe'** (round), **'French Breakfast'** (finger-like), **'Large White Icicle'** (long).

RUBY CHARD

A variety of Leaf Beet which can be grown as a decorative foliage plant. The leaves grow about 18 in. (45 cm) high — the fleshy leaf stalks and veins are red. A similar plant (Swiss Chard) has white stalks and veins. Sow seed 1 in. deep in April in the centre of a pot or tub. Pull off outer leaves when they are large enough for kitchen use — cook like Spinach. Variety: **'Ruby Chard'**.

Ruby Chard

Runner Bean 'Pickwick'

RUNNER BEAN

The Runner Bean earns its place as a container plant as it is a brightly coloured focal point when in full flower and a vegetable when the pods form. The standard varieties are grown as stick beans and allowed to climb, reaching 8 ft (240 cm) or more if unchecked. A few can be grown as ground beans (see below) by pinching out the growing points when the stems are 12 in. (30 cm) high. There are also dwarfs, growing only 18 in. (45 cm) high. For stick beans make sure that a stout support is provided — see page 115. Sow seed 2 in. deep in end May–early June. Pick regularly once the pods have reached a decent size (6–8 in. or 15–20 cm) but before the beans inside have started to swell. Varieties: **'Mergoles'**, **'Painted Lady'** (stick beans), **'Scarlet Emperor'**, **'Sunset'** (ground beans), **'Hammond's Dwarf Scarlet'**, **'Pickwick'** (dwarf beans).

TOMATO

It is worth trying to grow a few Tomato plants if you have a sheltered but sunny spot. It is fun to pick fruits straight from the plant and the flavour is generally better than greenhouse-grown ones. There are two basic types. The Cordon varieties are grown as single stems and they have to be trimmed and supported. The stem is stopped after the 4th truss has set so as to hasten ripening. There are many standard-sized red varieties — it is better to choose a Cherry variety for its bite-sized fruits with outstanding flavour or a Novelty variety for its yellow or striped fruits. Sow seed under glass in April and plant out in early June — set out 2 or 3 seedlings per growing bag. Follow the same sowing and planting times for the Bush varieties which make outdoor Tomato growing so much simpler. They are either bushy plants 12–30 in. (30–75 cm) high for pots, tubs, troughs, growing bags etc or trailers 9 in. (22.5 cm) long for hanging baskets. Varieties: **'Gardener's Delight'**, **'Sweet 100'** (Cordon, Cherry-fruited), **'Tigerella'**, **'Golden Sunrise'** (Cordon, Novelty-fruited), **'Sigmabush'**, **'Totem'** (bushy), **'Tumbler'** (trailer).

PLANT TYPE:
FRUIT

Vegetables and fruit are lumped together as food crops, but there are some basic differences. Most of the fruit types remain in the container for years whereas the vegetables are annuals — this means that repotting, top-dressing and winter protection are important considerations. Another difference is that some fruit trees are decorative in their own right whereas only a few vegetables are ornamental.

A few generalisations. Fruit trees appreciate a free root-run and do not like too much restriction — Apples, Pears, Cherries, Plums etc need a container which is at least 15 in. (37.5 cm) deep. Use a soil-based rather than a peat compost. Water thoroughly and regularly in summer but watering should not be needed in winter. Use netting as necessary for protection against frost and birds. A container-grown fruit tree on the patio is exposed to closer inspection than a similar specimen in the garden, so proper pruning and plant health measures are essential — see The Fruit Expert for details.

A range of fruit types are listed on the following pages and some are more satisfactory for container cultivation than others. If you want to choose just two plants to grow, then the top (tree) fruit should be Apple and the soft fruit type should be Strawberry.

APPLE

The introduction of dwarfing rootstocks such as M27 and M9 has made the cultivation of miniature Apple trees in containers a practical proposition — the main trunk will be about 2–3 ft (60–90 cm) high. Choose a 2 year old plant — one will do if it is a 'family' tree with 3–4 compatible varieties grafted on to it, or you may need to buy 2 or 3 different varieties for successful pollination if Apple trees are not common in your area. Plant in a deep pot or container and stake firmly. Allow only 2 or 3 fruit to develop in the first year — when mature the tree should produce about 10 lb (4.5 kg) annually. Train as a dwarf pyramid (see The Fruit Expert) and protect the container during very cold weather in winter. Varieties: **'Blenheim Orange'**, **'Discovery'**, **'Egremont Russett'**, **'Fiesta'**, **'Gala'**, **'Greensleeves'**, **'James Grieve'**, **'Sunset'**. A different approach is to grow a compact columnar tree which has a single trunk and hardly any side branches — they are sold as Ballerina or Minarette trees.

BLUEBERRY

These large blue-black berries are very popular in the U.S and are now available in greengrocers and supermarkets in Britain. It makes an excellent container plant as long as the tub or pot is at least 18 in. (45 cm) deep and an ericaceous peat compost is used. The bushes are self-fertile so you need only one — it will grow about 4 ft (120 cm) high, producing pink-tinged white flowers in spring, fruit in summer and bright red leaves in autumn. Use rainwater or soft tap water in dry weather — use netting when fruit starts to ripen. Variety: **'Bluecrop'**.

CHERRY

Most Cherries are far too vigorous to be grown in a container but the introduction of a dwarfing rootstock and a compact variety means that you can now grow a Cherry tree in a large tub in the same way as an Apple. Variety: There is just one — **'Compact Stella'** grafted on to Colt or Inmil rootstock. The flowers are self-fertile and the fruit is dark red.

Apple 'Gala'

Fig 'White Marseilles'

Grape 'Black Hamburgh'

Peach 'Duke of York'

Pear 'Conference'

CURRANT

Red Currants are tart but White Currants have a Grape-like flavour. Many varieties of Red and White Currant can be grown in containers — choose an upright, compact variety. Buy 2 year old plants and train as a bush or cordon. Like Gooseberries these Currants bear their fruit on stubby side-shoots (spurs) which arise on the older branches, so don't expect any fruit in the first year. Netting against birds while the fruit is still green is essential. Varieties: **'Red Lake'**, **'Stanza'** (red), **'White Versailles'** (white).

FIG

Unlike many other fruit trees Figs benefit from having their roots restricted, which means that they make good container plants. Plant in spring in a large tub and place against a south- or south west-facing wall. Train as a small bush and look after its fussy needs — read The Fruit Expert. Tiny fruits formed at the end of summer develop into next year's Figs, so protect them from frost in winter. A Fig is ready for picking when the stalk weakens and the fully-coloured fruit hangs downwards. Repot in late winter every 2–3 years. Varieties: **'Brown Turkey'**, **'White Marseilles'**.

GOOSEBERRY

Gooseberries can be grown in containers and will do well in sun or semi-shade. The sweet dessert varieties can be grown, but the Gooseberry is not a popular tub plant. The thorns make pruning troublesome, birds eat the developing fruits and spraying is often necessary to prevent serious pest and disease damage. Buy a 2 or 3 year old plant if you want to try this crop and train it as a bush, half standard or fan. Varieties: **'Jubilee'**, **'May Duke'**, **'Golden Drop'**.

GRAPES

Grapes are the opposite to Figs — they dislike root restriction and are never really happy in pots or tubs. Still, there is something especially appealing about having a vine festooned with bunches of Grapes on the patio or porch, so it may be worth trying if you have a south-facing wall. Choose a dessert variety and plant in March — training and regular pruning are essential if you are to avoid a plant with masses of foliage and very few bunches of fruit. Use the cordon training system — see The Fruit Expert. Netting will be necessary to protect the fruit — but you can't expect any fruit until 3 years after planting. Outdoor varieties are often grown for wine-making as there is rarely enough sunshine to develop sweet and juicy flesh. Varieties: **'Brandt'**, **'Black Hamburgh'**, **'Foster's Seedling'**, **'Siegerrebe'**.

PEACH

Peach trees can be grown successfully against south-facing walls in areas with a favourable climate. Bushes are the easiest growth type to care for and they give the highest yields, but fans grown against the wall benefit from the extra warmth and frost protection. If you want to take the risk of growing a Peach in a container then choose one of the hardier varieties listed below. The usual rootstock is St. Julien A but look for the dwarfing rootstock Pixy which will produce compact trees just 6–8 ft (180–240 cm) high. Cover the flowers with sacking or netting in spring to protect them from frost and net the plants again in summer to protect the fruit from birds. The blooms are self-fertile but will need hand pollination. Varieties: **'Peregrine'**, **'Duke of York'**.

PEAR

Pear is a much poorer choice than Apple as a tree fruit for a container. There are no dwarfing rootstocks — even the most restricting one will produce a tree which will grow 8 ft (240 cm) high or more. A container 2 ft (60 cm) deep is required, and you will need to plant 2 varieties as Pears need pollination partners. Buy a 2 year old bush and train it as a dwarf pyramid. Prune and protect in the same way as Apples — see page 87. Varieties: **'Conference'**, **'Beth'**, **'Concorde'**. A different approach is to grow a compact columnar tree which has a single trunk and hardly any branches, sold as a Minarette tree.

PLUM

This stone fruit is easy to grow — it is hardy and there are several self-fertile varieties from which you can make your choice. The problem is that the flowers appear early in the season and this means that pollination can be disappointing. Birds can be a problem — both buds in spring and fruit in summer are at risk. Buy a 2 or 3 year old partly-trained tree on Pixy rootstock. Grow as a fan against a south-facing wall or as a bush. Festooning is often recommended for container-grown Plums — the branches are bent over and tied to the main stem to form a mushroom-like crown. A word of caution — never prune in winter. Varieties: **'Victoria'**, **'Denniston's Superb'**.

RASPBERRY

If you are really keen on fresh Raspberries and do not have a garden then you can grow canes in a large tub. The ordinary summer-fruiting Raspberry, however, is not a good container plant — the tall canes are not attractive and require support, and protection against birds is essential. Grow instead an autumn-fruiting variety. Fruiting starts in August and goes on until the first frosts, and neither support nor netting is essential. Pruning is simple — cut down all the canes to the compost level in February. Varieties: **'Autumn Bliss'**, **'Zeva'** (red), **'Fall Gold'** (yellow).

STRAWBERRY

It is not surprising that the Strawberry is the queen of the container fruits and is more widely grown than all the other types put together. You don't need a lot of room — you can grow them in ordinary sized pots, tubs, troughs, growing bags, window boxes and hanging baskets. You also don't need a lot of patience — plant in August and you can pick in June or July next year. The flowers and fruits are attractive, but there are cultural as well as decorative and space-saving benefits. The fruit is kept away from slugs and picking is made easier. Mulching and hoeing are not necessary and protection involves simply draping a net over the container. The popular varieties are the summer-fruiting ones, cropping late May–late July. With any one type the fruiting period lasts for only a couple of weeks — extend this by planting perpetual varieties as well, which crop in late summer and autumn. When planting a strawberry barrel (page 20) follow the procedure outlined for a chicken wire tower on page 34. Replant the container every 2–3 years. Varieties: **'Cambridge Favourite'**, **'Tamella'**, **'Bounty'** (summer-fruiting), **'Gento'**, **'Rapella'**, **'Aromel'** (perpetual).

Plum 'Victoria'

Raspberry 'Fall Gold'

PLANT TYPE:
HERBS

The culinary (pot) herbs which are used for flavouring food are suitable for container growing — pots of Mint, Rosemary, Thyme etc have been a feature of cottage windowsills for hundreds of years. The range on offer these days at garden centres is large and it is impossible to generalise about growth habit or the most suitable container. At one end of the scale is the Bay Laurel (page 61) which is a tree requiring a large pot or tub — at the other end are the ground-hugging varieties of Thyme. Planting one variety with other types of herbs or bedding plants in a trough, growing bag or window box is practical but not always a good idea — some herbs are invasive and soon swamp more delicate plants. Perhaps the best plan is to grow herbs in a group of pots, a herb wheel (page 92) or a herb pot (page 20).

Most types can be raised from seed but it is more practical to buy them as small plants in pots from the garden centre. With shrubby herbs such as Rosemary you will need only a single plant but with smaller herbaceous herbs like Parsley and Chives you will need several specimens.

Site the herb container close to the house and harvest them at the proper growth stage. Pick your requirements for immediate use when the plants are actively growing between spring and autumn, and also pick some for drying.

Basil

Chives

BASIL
Ht: 9 in. (22.5 cm)

This tender annual cannot stand frost. Sow under glass in a peat pot in March or April and plant out in early June in a sunny spot. Pinch out the growing tips to produce a bushy plant. During the summer gather leaves as required — the best way to have Basil for winter is to lift plants and pot up in September, placing the pots on the kitchen windowsill. The Clove-like flavour of Basil is an essential feature of many Italian recipes and its traditional partner is the Tomato.

CHERVIL
Ht: 15 in. (37.5 cm)

Chervil is a hardy herb which grows quickly — the first leaves can be picked 8 weeks after sowing and it can be used in winter. Sow Chervil where it is to grow — a March sowing will provide a summer crop and an August sowing will provide leaves from autumn to spring. Thin to leave seedlings 6 in. (15 cm) apart — remove leaves from the outside of the plant when harvesting. Take off the seed-heads. Chervil has ferny leaves with an Aniseed flavour which can be lost by cooking — add finely chopped leaves to soups, fish and egg dishes just before serving.

CHIVES
Ht: 12 in. (30 cm)

The grass-like stems can be cut from March to October to improve the flavour of many dishes, but dried Chives are of little value. Plant pot-grown clumps in spring or autumn 9 in. apart and divide every 3 or 4 years. Cut the stems to within an inch or two of compost level. Remove the flower buds before they open if you grow it purely as a herb with a mild Garlic-Onion flavour, but it can be used as an attractive flowering plant from which some leaves are removed for the kitchen. Finely chopped Chives are used in many ways — in potato salad, stuffed eggs, omelettes, sauces, soups etc.

DILL
***Ht:** 24 in. (60 cm)*

A tall annual herb which has attractive feathery foliage and flat plates of small yellow flowers in July. It hates disturbance — sow the seeds in April where the plants are to grow and thin to 12 in. (30 cm) apart. Gather leaves for immediate use and for drying while they are still young — the distinct flavour is retained after drying. Harvest and dry the seeds once the flower-heads have turned brown — tie a paper bag over each flower-head and hang stems upside-down. Use chopped leaves as a garnish or in the cooking of all types of fish — the strongly-flavoured seeds are used in rice as well as fish dishes.

FENNEL
***Ht:** up to 48 in. (120 cm)*

If you grow herbs in pots of different sizes then Fennel should be in the back row — this tall and attractive perennial has blue-green feathery foliage and flat heads of tiny yellow flowers in summer. There is a purple-leaved variety which is even more decorative. Buy a pot-grown plant from the garden centre or nursery and choose a sunny spot. Pick leaves in summer as required. Remove the taller shoots bearing flower buds if you do not intend to collect the seeds for drying — harvest the seeds in the way described for Dill. Fennel is interchangeable with Dill — use the chopped foliage for fish, salads, vegetables and soups. The seeds are used to flavour oily fish.

Fennel

MARJORAM
***Ht:** 15 in. (37.5 cm)*

Sweet Marjoram is a half hardy annual — seed is sown under glass in March and planted out in the container at the end of May. In autumn the plants are lifted and put into pots on the windowsill to provide a winter supply of leaves. It is better to grow Pot Marjoram — buy a pot-grown specimen in spring and plant in a container where it will grow as readily as Mint. This small-leaved shrub is a perennial, although the foliage usually dies down in winter. Cut back dead stems in spring. The prime use of chopped Marjoram is for sprinkling over meat or poultry before roasting.

Mint

MINT
***Ht:** up to 24 in. (60 cm)*

This robust invasive perennial is one of our favourite herbs. There are several varieties, such as the highly fragrant Apple Mint, the highly flavoured Bowles Mint and the common-or-garden Spearmint. Variegated-leaved varieties are available. All produce spikes of tiny pink or pale purple flowers. Plant a piece of root 2 in. deep in sun or light shade. Lift and divide every 3 years. If mint rust appears (orange spots on shoots), dig up and burn the plants. Mint is used when boiling new Potatoes and Peas, but its most popular use is as the basic ingredient in mint sauce.

PARSLEY
***Ht:** 9 in. (22.5 cm)*

The bright green and deeply-divided leaves of Parsley provide our most popular garnish. The curly-leaved varieties are the most decorative and the plain-leaved ones have the strongest flavour. Sow seed ½ in. deep in April for a summer or autumn crop — germination is very slow so you may prefer to buy young plants in pots. Pick regularly to ensure a continuous supply — remove flowering stems as they appear. Cover overwintering plants with straw or peat. Parsley can be grown in a special parsley pot — see page 20. There are many uses — garnishing dishes, enriching white sauce, making *bouquet garni* etc. To dry Parsley dip sprigs in boiling water for 2 minutes and then crisp in a cool oven.

Parsley

ROSEMARY
***Ht:** up to 36 in. (90 cm)*

This attractive evergreen shrub is slightly tender — grow it close to a south-facing wall. Plant up a pot-grown specimen in spring — pick regularly and trim the bushes to keep them about 24 in. (60 cm) high. Both the needle-like foliage and the small blue flowers are highly aromatic and suitable for kitchen use. Winter frosts may kill some of the shoots but new growth will sprout from the base. Variegated types are less hardy than ordinary green Rosemary. Plants become leggy with age — renew every 3 years. Rosemary is the traditional flavouring for lamb, pork and veal — use sparingly.

Rosemary

Sage

Summer Savory

SAGE

Ht: *up to 24 in. (60 cm)*

A bush which is ornamental as well as useful as a herb — the oblong grey-green leaves are wrinkled and the flower spikes bear tubular violet-blue flowers. Plant a pot-grown specimen in spring in a sunny spot — gather the leaves regularly and trim the bush lightly in July after flowering. The leaves can be dried for winter use — harvest them for this purpose in late spring. It is not a long-lived plant — renew every 3 years. Sage and its partner Onion are the traditional ingredients in the stuffing for duck and goose, but there are many other uses.

SAVORY

Ht: *9 in. (22.5 cm)*

Some of the herbs in this section are known by everybody, but Savory is not. There are two types. Summer Savory is an annual — the leaves are picked before the flowers appear and again when the new leaves develop after the flower stems have been cut back. Winter Savory is a low-growing evergreen perennial — plant in April and trim back in early spring every year. Both types have narrow leaves and small tubular flowers, and both are used in salads or egg dishes or as a substitute for Sage when making stuffing.

TARRAGON

Ht: *24 in. (60 cm)*

Tarragon is an invasive perennial which spreads like Mint. The greyish-green leaves are aromatic and the tiny flowers are greenish-yellow. Plant a pot-grown specimen in March and pick leaves between June and October. Remove flowering shoots to maintain the supply of fresh leaves. The foliage dies down in winter — the underground runners produce a fresh crop of leaves each spring. Make sure you buy French and not Russian Tarragon. Tarragon is a basic feature of French cooking and is used in many classical chicken and fish dishes.

THYME

Ht: *9 in. (22.5 cm)*

Thyme is a low-growing spreading shrub which is strongly aromatic. It is evergreen, so the shoots with their tiny leaves can be picked all year round. There are numerous varieties, including the strongly-flavoured Common Thyme, the citrus-flavoured Lemon Thyme as well as the decorative variegated and yellow-leaved varieties. Plant pot-grown specimens in spring — do not let the plants flower. Lift and divide every 3–4 years. Thyme has many uses — it is the traditional partner for Parsley in the stuffing for poultry.

CHAPTER 4
ARRANGING CONTAINERS

So far in this book we have dealt with the surprisingly large selection of containers now available and also the numerous types of plants which can be used to fill them. These are two basic ingredients of the overall design — the third key element is the siting of the container or containers.

Container, plants, situation — good design involves arranging these three features so that an attractive visual impact is coupled with good growing conditions for the plants. This rarely happens by accident — the secret is careful planning.

What do you want to achieve? This first question is vital — if it is just a bright splash of colour then a single pot, tub or hanging basket may well serve your purpose, but to brighten a dull wall or a bare patio you may have to think about a group of containers. Your object may be much more down to earth — if you want to grow plants for the kitchen or wish to house a treasured collection then the appearance of the container is much less important than the plant material. Strictly formal or chintzy informal, permanent or seasonal planting, unassuming or dramatic — these are questions to answer before you begin.

Having decided on the object of the display, think about the space to be occupied by the planted-up container — **the size of the container should be in proportion to the surroundings**. A tiny pot on a large expanse of paving can look as out of place as a large ornate urn in a small and simple plot. Balance is also necessary, and this is largely governed by the relation of the plants to the container. The basic rule is that **the display should neither look as if it would blow over in the wind nor need an earthquake to shift it**. A tall and narrow container with a tall upright plant and no trailers can look distinctly unstable whereas a low bowl filled with carpeting annuals can look too solid and bottom heavy.

After size and balance you should think about visual impact. As a general rule you should **choose whether to make the container or the plants the main focus of interest**. A simple arrangement in a highly decorative pot will highlight the beauty of the container, whereas a plain tub or simple hanging basket will not detract from the impact of an impressive floral display. However, this concept of making either the container or the plants the main feature is only a general and not a universal rule — attractive displays are often created with lively plant arrangements in a decorated container. The two pitfalls to avoid are the display where neither pot nor planting has any impact and the display where both pot and planting are highly colourful and/or dramatically ornate.

When considering size, balance and visual impact you will undoubtedly have been thinking about the choice of plants. Colour is a basic factor here, and it is important that you should not think that a multi-hued display is necessary or even the best choice in many situations. A single colour or subtle blend is often preferable — see the examples on page 98. There are no 'right' colours — some people prefer the warm colours (reds, yellows etc) which make the flowers look closer and others like the cool colours (blues, greens etc) which make the display look further away. There is, however, one rule of thumb about colour — you should **choose hues which will make the display stand out, so pick brightly coloured plants against a dark background and deep and vibrant hues against pale surroundings**. Note that this need for contrast applies to the plant/background relationship and not to the plant/container one.

The aspects dealt with so far (size, balance, visual impact and colour) are all important design considerations, and there are several others. One is the absence of obstruction — avoid at all costs turning a patio, path or stairway into an obstacle course by badly siting containers. Another important aspect is the way to group containers together. There are no firm rules here, but if you are in doubt and don't trust your own design sense then **group pots, tubs etc together rather than scattering them about, have an odd number in the group and aim for some variety of sizes and shapes**. Not too much variety, though — aim for some linkage by having the same varieties growing in some of the containers or by using trailing plants which straddle neighbouring pots.

Balance

◁ A tall and narrow container such as a chimney pot or bowl on a pedestal needs to be given an air of stability when planted. You can have a compact arrangement to give the impression of visual balance or you can use trailing plants as in the photograph to avoid a top-heavy look. The Petunias are quite tall, but the Ivy and Glechoma give the display a stable appearance

A squat tub such as a shallow half-barrel can look distinctly bottom-heavy if planted with a selection of low-growing plants. This display has been given a balanced look by planting Cannas as dot plants at the centre. These plants provide the necessary height to offset the compact nature of the types chosen as filler plants ▷

A chimney pot with a tall plant may be ▷
physically balanced, which means that
the weight of compost and container
would prevent it from falling over.
However, it will still look unstable and
top-heavy — it lacks visual balance.
This display in a chimney pot would be
much improved if some edging plants
and trailers had been planted around
the column-like conifer

◁ A large and heavy urn or trough
generally needs one or more tall plants
to prevent the display looking bottom-
heavy like this Snowdrop planting in a
stone urn. Do not take this as a
universal rule — troughs are
sometimes used to make attractive
alpine gardens and a low-growing
group in a bowl can be dramatic... if
you have the eye of a skilled designer

Visual Impact

◁ *The ornate modelling of this Brannam cherub pot would have been lost if vigorous trailers had been planted or would have been diminished if a polychromatic mixture of bedding plants had been grown. The simple planting of a single Geranium variety has left the pot as the main feature*

Here the tub is an unattractive cylinder ▷ of plain concrete. In this case it was necessary to ensure that the planting display and not the container should be the centre of interest. A massed planting of Geranium, Allysum, Lobelia and Helichrysum in and around the tub has provided the necessary contrast to the dull container surface

If you look closely at this display you will ▷
see that the container is an attractive
octagonal Gothic urn with a series of
quatrefoil panels. The planting of dainty
white Roses is excellent, but the mass of
variegated Ivy leaves has almost
completely hidden the ornate modelling
of this reconstituted stone container

◁ Here a converted container has been
used — a stack of white-painted tyres.
The basic planting of Polyanthus is
colourful enough, but nothing has been
done to cover the glaring surface of
the tyres which most people would find
unattractive. The planting should
definitely dominate here, and this calls
for leafy trailers such as Ivy, Glechoma,
Helichrysum, Nasturtium, Petunia
'Surfinia' etc

Colour

◁ **MONOCHROMATIC SCHEME**

In a monochromatic scheme the various tints and shades of a single colour are used. The visual effect of a container can be heightened by the simplicity of such a planting. Simple, but it need not be monotonous if you use a wide range of the basic colour — for example pink Petunias, blood red Geraniums and maroon Antirrhinums in a pot or bowl. White and yellow are popular choices — blue is the most difficult as the range is limited

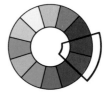

◁ **ANALOGOUS SCHEME**

In an analogous (or related) scheme, the two, three or four colours used are all neighbours on the colour wheel. Such an arrangement has much of the subdued charm of a monochromatic scheme but there is of course a much larger range of plants from which to make a choice. Here reds and violets have been used, ranging from pale pink to deep violet. White flowers or silvery foliage can be used to brighten an analogous scheme

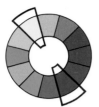

CONTRASTING SCHEME ▷

In a contrasting (or complementary) scheme the chosen colours are directly across from each other on the colour wheel. For maximum impact the pure colours rather than pastel tints should be used — yellow Marigolds and violet Lobelias as in the illustration, bright orange Antirrhinums and blue Scaveola, and so on. The effect, however, may be garish and so tints and shades of the basic colours are often preferred

POLYCHROMATIC SCHEME ▷

In a polychromatic (or rainbow) scheme colours from all parts of the colour wheel are used — a patchwork quilt of reds, violets, yellows, oranges etc. This was once everybody's idea of a hanging basket and is still widely used in pots, tubs, window boxes and so on, but there is a distinct movement away from polychromatic schemes these days and the appeal of simplicity is taking hold

Planting

◁ SINGLE VARIETY

The single variety plays an important role in container gardening. There may be just one specimen plant — the Hydrangea or Bay Laurel in a tub or the single Hosta in a pot. With bulbs, bedding plants and vegetables a group rather than one plant is generally planted, as with the cluster of Tagetes patula 'Pascal' in the photograph

VARIETIES OF A SINGLE GENUS ▷

Where more varied colour is required than can be obtained with a single variety it is quite usual to grow varieties or species of a single genus. A multicoloured mixture of Universal Pansies for winter or Polyanthus for spring are both popular. The plants may have a different growth habit — here Bedding Geraniums (Pelargonium hortorum) have been planted with trailing Ivy-leaved Geraniums (P. peltatum)

PLANTS OF THE
SAME TYPE

▷

A collection of different plants belonging to the same main type (see page 41) is by far the most popular planting arrangement for containers. The collection of bedding plants in a pot, trough, window box or hanging basket is the prime example, but you will also find rockery perennials in troughs, aquatic plants in miniponds and spring-flowering bulbs in tubs

◁ ## PLANTS OF
DIFFERENT TYPES

This planting arrangement is much less usual than the scheme described above, although spring bulbs and spring-flowering bedding plants are often grown together. Another example is the bedding scheme planting where a dwarf conifer is a central permanent feature. In the illustration the situation is reversed — the permanent planting of Pieris, Euonymus and Ivy are the main feature and Pansies are used to provide a few spots of seasonal colour

Grouping

△ SINGLE CONTAINER

There are many situations where a group of containers can add an expanse of colour and interest which would be impossible with a single pot, tub or urn, but as a focal point the single impressive container is often the preferred choice. A good example is illustrated here. A strip of Feverfew (Chrysanthemum parthenium 'Aureum') leads up to the Haddonstone gothic jardiniere which has been planted with the same variety, turning the reconstituted stone container into a dramatic focal point

PAIRED CONTAINERS ▷

A pair of containers planted in the same way provides an excellent framing device where a formal look is required — on either side of a door, window, flight of stairs, pathway etc. Box trees in tubs, bedding plants in urns and brightly coloured hanging baskets are popular examples — good in the right situation but a poor choice in informal, cottagey surroundings

◁ SCATTERED CONTAINERS

This is the container arrangement to be found in millions of gardens — a window box here, a few hanging baskets there, a pot or two on the patio and a few other containers around the house. There is nothing basically wrong with this arrangement, but it can look 'bitty' if all the containers and their plants are different, and watering every day in dry weather can be laborious

Grouping continued

◁ **THE SMALL GROUP**
It is the small group which will test your design skills — the arrangement, container materials and plant choice are all-important. In this example you will see the triangular arrangement recommended by the experts, with the Cordyline forming the apex. You will also see the interest created by an empty jar or two, but it would have been improved, perhaps, if all the pots had been terracotta

THE MASSED GROUP ▷
Here it is the planting which is usually dominant — the containers are often hidden. You will see this arrangement in all sorts of situations — a large collection of pots in a dull corner, balcony boxes covering the front of European homes etc. In the extreme example illustrated here the front of a town house has been transformed with window boxes, hanging baskets, pots, troughs and urns

GROUPING OF SIMILAR CONTAINERS ▷

Similar containers planted with the same variety are used to give a feeling of unity. The front of this large house and its annexe needed something to tie the parts together — a line of evenly spaced terracotta jars planted with Hydrangeas has been used for this purpose. Size is not a basic requirement — this type of arrangement can be valuable in a tiny garden

◁ **GROUPING OF DIFFERENT CONTAINERS**

The role of a group of dissimilar containers with a variety of planting schemes is to create a centre of interest. Monotony must be avoided, but there should be at least one unifying feature. Here all the Apta pots and jars are made of terracotta and three of them are planted with yellow Chrysanthemums. Note, however, that this is only a general rule which the experts sometimes ignore!

Front Door

The simplest approach to using
containers near a doorway is to use
a single unit — a hanging basket, a
specimen tree or a pot filled with
bedding plants. Here Violas have
been used in a fibre pot to provide a
bright splash of colour ▷

◁ Containers can be used to frame the
doorway rather than providing a single focal
point. The arrangement can be formal and
neatly symmetrical or informal and clearly
asymmetrical. The popular formal approach
is to have paired hanging baskets, as
illustrated, or paired tubs

△ This arrangement is in sharp contrast to the balanced
example above — there is a lop-sided look with a standard
Bay Laurel on one side and Double Daisies on the other

Window

*Several containers have been used here ▷
to frame and decorate this window.
Hanging baskets, a window box and a
wall-mounted pot have all been employed
— which may seem to be too much for
many people*

◁ *To increase the impact of the display it is
often better to have a double window box
arrangement than scattered containers.
Note how closely the plantings have been
linked so as to avoid a discordant note.
Again this may seem to be over the top*

△ *The classical way of decorating a window is to fix a window box below it and
plant up with flowers and/or foliage plants which do not seriously reduce the
view. Bedding plants are by far the most popular planting material*

Balcony

△ *The beauty of the decorated balcony can be commonly seen in many European countries such as Germany, Austria, Switzerland etc but not in Britain. All too often we decorate the walls with hanging baskets and the paved areas with tubs and troughs, but ignore the balcony itself. This photograph shows how stunning the effect can be when both the top and bottom of the balcony carry a line of troughs which are filled with a single variety of Geraniums*

Steps

◁ The living balustrade is a useful design feature if you have a flight of open-sided steps in the garden. It is usual but not essential to have a series of identical pots and plantings — in this example the containers match the steps and only the uppermost one is different in size. Each pot is planted with Box which has been trimmed to create an evergreen balustrade

An alternative approach to having ▷ containers at the side of each step is to have a display to frame either the top or the bottom of the flight of steps. Bedding plants or bulbs in pots and standard trees or clipped evergreens in tubs are popular choices. A more lavish arrangement is to have a massed display which frames the whole flight of steps, as illustrated here

Patio

◁ One of the two basic approaches to using containers on a patio or in a courtyard is to place a single planted-up specimen so as to add interest to an area of dull paving. Here an ornamental pot has been used, but the key feature is still the display of Argyranthemum and Felicia blooms. Several scattered containers are sometimes used in this way on a large patio — care is needed not to hinder free passage

The other approach is to use a display ▷ which creates an area of living texture and colour against a dull background. This background may be a bare or unsightly part of the garden or it may be a plain wall. In this example a massed display has been arranged against a shaded courtyard wall. Note the unifying techniques here — similar Geraniums have been used in different pots and the colours have been restricted to white, pinks and reds

CHAPTER 5
CARING FOR CONTAINERS

Containers have their own special charm compared with beds and borders, but they also have their own special needs. When the weather turns dry during the growing season then thorough and regular watering is essential, and once the food supply in the compost is exhausted then feeding is required. But proper care calls for more than just watering and feeding — many plants require regular dead-heading, some need staking or a similar form of support and overwintering plants may call for special protection.

The various sections in this chapter will give you the general principles involved in container care, but there are very few hard and fast rules which apply to all plants, all containers and all situations. The reason is that the correct type and timing of treatment will depend on the weather, compost, size and material of the container, type of plant or plants, location and time of year.

It has been said several times on earlier pages that plants in containers are more closely inspected than those growing in beds and borders. So top-grade plants are essential, but even the most expensive and vigorous planted-up specimens will soon look bedraggled if they are not properly tended. This means that there are things to learn and jobs to do, but the work involved is not usually strenuous nor is it really time-consuming as the area devoted to containers is generally quite small. The end result will be a display which makes the little extra effort well worthwhile.

DEAD-HEADING

The removal of dead flowers has several advantages — it helps to give the container a well-maintained look, it prolongs the floral display and in a few cases it may induce a second flush of flowers late in the season. Use secateurs, finger nails or shears — take care not to tear the stalk and do not remove too much stem and foliage when dead-heading.

Dead-heading is a vital task with many bedding plants. If flowers are left to go to seed then part of the plant's energy is wasted, but a much more important fact is that seed formation may produce a flower-blocking hormone within the plant. So do dead-head Pansies, Petunias and Geraniums if you can, but for some bedding plants it is either not needed or not worth carrying out. Sterile plants such as Afro-French Marigolds do not set seed so dead-heading is merely a tidying-up operation — with tiny-flowered types like Lobelia it is not practical to cut off every dead bloom. Lobelia does have a longer flowering season if the tops are removed after the first flush, but some types (e.g Begonia and Impatiens) produce flowers all season long even if not dead-headed. Some shrubs (e.g Rose and Camellia) should be dead-headed to prolong the flowering season.

PRUNING

Some pruning generally takes place during the season in the well-tended container. With bedding plants this starts at an early stage — either before or just after planting out. The growing point plus a small amount of stem is nipped out between finger and thumb — a procedure known as pinching out. It stimulates bud production lower down the stem and side shoots are thus produced — this is the way to make plants such as Antirrhinum, Coleus, Salvia etc bushy.

Dead-heading is a form of pruning, but some annuals need more drastic action. Some like Petunia have straggly stems which need cutting back in order to stay attractive. Others such as Helichrysum and Nasturtium need cutting back so that they will not swamp more delicate types.

Shrubs grown for their foliage usually need little pruning apart from the removal of weak and unwanted branches. With all trees and shrubs it is necessary to trim to maintain an attractive shape but with flowering types it is necessary to follow the instructions in The Flowering Shrub Expert — haphazard snipping during the growing season can mean no flowers next year.

WATERING

The task of watering is more time-consuming than any other aspect of container growing and it is probably the most difficult to master. You must never allow watering to become a regular routine, such as every weekend in winter and every other day in summer. The correct timing will depend on many factors — a partial list includes the season of the year, recent rainfall, size and type of container, temperature, location and compost type. As a result of these factors a hanging basket in a sunny exposed spot in summer may need watering twice a day when the weather is dry whereas a pot will need no water at all during a rainy spell in winter.

Because of these variable factors there can be no clear-cut specific rules, but there are a number of points for general guidance. Among the basic things to remember is that roots need air as well as water, which means that the compost must be dampened all the way through when watering, but there should be a short period of drying out at the surface before the next watering. The time interval between waterings will depend on many factors as noted above — the way to tell when you should water is noted on page 113. To increase the time interval between waterings you should choose a large non-porous container, grow shrubs, use a soil-based compost and pick a sheltered site. Do not try to cut down the need for frequent watering by standing the container in a water-filled tray. Finally, don't assume that rain will always do the job for you — very little rain may get to the compost in a window box under projecting eaves or to the compost in a pot where the plant leaves form a dense cover all over the surface.

WATERING TOO OFTEN or POOR DRAINAGE

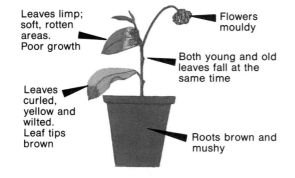

Leaves limp; soft, rotten areas. Poor growth

Flowers mouldy

Both young and old leaves fall at the same time

Leaves curled, yellow and wilted. Leaf tips brown

Roots brown and mushy

NOT WATERING OFTEN ENOUGH

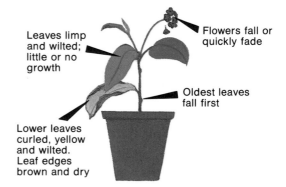

Leaves limp and wilted; little or no growth

Flowers fall or quickly fade

Oldest leaves fall first

Lower leaves curled, yellow and wilted. Leaf edges brown and dry

HOLIDAY CARE

Your time for rest and relaxation away from home in summer may be a time of decline or even death for your plants in containers. The most satisfactory solution is to persuade a friend to call and look after them. If you can't find a plant babysitter then you should create the illustrated set-up. Move the containers if you can to a shady spot and place a large bowl filled with water on some form of support above them. Run a length of wick, strip of capillary matting or other sort of absorbent cloth from the bottom of the bowl to the compost surface in each container — push the wick below the surface.

WHEN TO WATER

Do not make the plants beg for water by drooping their leaves and stem tips — water before wilting takes place. The simplest technique is to look at the surface — daily in summer, weekly in winter. If the surface is dry all over, insert your finger tip. It is time to water if the compost is dry down to the length of your finger nail in a small container or down to 1 in. (2.5 cm) in a large one. Never allow a peat-based compost to dry out more than this — once dried out this type of compost shrinks and is difficult to rewet as illustrated below. Some people use a moisture meter to tell them when to water, but the finger nail test is adequate. Water in the morning or evening — try to avoid watering when the sun is shining brightly. Never water when the weather is frosty.

Do not apply a daily dribble — this can do more harm than good. Fill the watering space completely and let it drain through the holes. Growing bags are a special case — you can't just fill a watering space and leave it to drain. Read and follow the manufacturer's instructions. The methods and timing of watering for bags filled with soil-based, peat-based and coir-based compost are different — note carefully the technique which is recommended when changing from one compost to another.

HOW TO WATER

If you have just a few containers then a **long-spouted watering can** will do — pour the water steadily and gently to fill the watering space. Where there are a number of assorted containers then a **hose pipe** will save you a lot of time. Having containers grouped together rather than scattered around the garden will also save time. Have an on-off trigger at the end of the hose. In hot dry weather watering with either a can or hose can be a daily task, so it is worth considering **self-watering containers** to cut down the work. These can be topped up as required at weekly intervals. Even easier but more expensive are the **automatic** and **semi-automatic systems** with small pipes running to each container — the supply may be manually- or computer-controlled. These systems are only worth considering if you have a long line of troughs or window boxes.

THE WATER TO USE

Tap water is suitable for nearly all plants, but do not use hard water on lime-haters such as Azalea, Cyclamen, Camellia and Rhododendron. Rainwater is excellent, but it must not be stagnant.

WATERING TROUBLES

WATER NOT ABSORBED

Cause: Surface caking
Cure: Prick over the surface with a fork or trowel. Then immerse the pot to compost level in a large receptacle filled with water

WATER RUNS STRAIGHT THROUGH

Cause: Shrinkage of compost away from the side of the pot
Cure: Immerse the pot to compost level in a large receptacle filled with water

WATERING OVERHEAD CONTAINERS

It has been stressed in this book that small containers will need frequent watering in hot and dry weather. This is a time-consuming but not difficult task in most cases, but it can be a problem with overhead containers such as hanging baskets and window boxes. It is possible to use steps and a watering can in some instances, but there are three alternatives which can make the task easier.

HOSE LANCE
Convenient with unlimited capacity — large areas can be covered. Difficult to direct accurately. Lances with fitted fertilizer applicators are now available

PUMP CAN
Neat and simple to use — no hose pipe is needed. Suitable if you have one or two hanging baskets to water but not practical for large areas

UP-DOWN MECHANISM
The basket is brought down to easy reach. Two types are available — a simple pulley on the bracket or a spring-loaded holder on the basket chain

FEEDING

A gardener soon learns that the production of stems, leaves, roots and flowers is a drain on the soil's reserves of plant foods. This effect is quite quickly seen with some plants —lawn grasses, leafy vegetables etc but the need for feeding may never be noticed, as with trees, rockery perennials etc.

The situation is quite different with plants growing in containers. In this environment *all* plants will suffer if a supply of nutrients is not made available to the roots. There are two reasons — the amount of compost is strictly limited so that the content of available nitrogen, phosphates, potash and trace elements is quite quickly exhausted, and the regular watering of the compost speeds up the process by washing away a proportion of these plant foods through the drainage holes. The answer is to use one of the fertilizer types listed below:

SOLUBLE or LIQUID FERTILIZER The most popular but not a long-lasting method. Feed when you water at 14 day intervals

POWDER or GRANULAR FERTILIZER Sprinkle it over the moist compost and prick into the surface. Longer lasting but slower acting than liquid fertilizer

FERTILIZER STICKS Pellets or sticks of compressed fertilizer are pushed into the compost as instructed. The feeding effect lasts for 2–3 months

FOLIAR FERTILIZER Spray on to leaves as instructed. Quick acting — use for supplying trace elements when deficiencies are seen

SLOW-RELEASE FERTILIZER Granules or cones of specially-coated fertilizer are sprinkled over or pushed into the compost. Lasts for 6 months

INJECTED FERTILIZER An effective way of applying dilute liquid fertilizer, but not popular. A perforated spike takes the solution to the roots

* A soil-based compost requires feeding less often than a peat- or coir-based one

* Use a high-nitrogen fertilizer for foliage plants and a high-potash feed for flowering and/or fruiting ones. Use a high-potash feed for a mixed collection

* Keep powder and granular fertilizers off leaves and flowers — wash with water if these parts are accidentally treated. Do not apply right up to the stems

* Make sure the compost is moist before applying a solid or liquid fertilizer. Water in any type of solid fertilizer after application

* Do not feed dormant perennials during the winter months — wait until growth starts in spring and stop when growth slows down in autumn

* Make sure that you use the amount recommended on the package. Double the amount does not give twice the benefit — it can lead to scorch

* Do not store fertilizer bags or cartons in a damp place. Always close the top after use and keep the packages off the floor. Store well away from weedkillers

TOP DRESSING

For a variety of reasons, especially with large pots and trained specimens, you may not wish or be able to disturb the plant by repotting. In this case the pot should be top dressed every spring. Carefully remove the top 1–2 in. (2.5–5 cm) of compost and loosen the surface with a hand fork. Replace this removed material with fresh compost.

STAKING & SUPPORTING

Climbers, plants with weak stems, tall varieties on exposed sites, large-headed flowers and young shrubs in containers close to a wall will all need some form of support, and care has to be taken to ensure that an attractive display is not ruined by ugly staking. The golden rule is to put the stake in position when the plant is quite small so that the stems can cover it.

For many plants brushwood is all you will need but for tall dot plants a stouter form of staking is required at planting time. The single bamboo cane method is sometimes used in deep containers, but with bushy plants an ugly 'drumstick' effect can be produced. It is better to use a circular support, cane wigwam or chicken-wire roll (see below) — but with standard trees the stout wooden stake and adjustable plastic ties are the recommended method of support.

These methods are designed for inserting in a free-standing container, but climbers grown against a wall will need a support which will enable part or all of the vertical surface to be clothed by the plant. The framework should be strong and new growth should be trained into it regularly.

With both free-standing and wall supports it is generally necessary to tie the stems to them. Soft twine and raffia are the traditional and still recommended materials and avoid tying too tightly. When training a climber on to a trellis, wires etc you should not tie the stems vertically — spread them at an angle to form a fan so as to increase the display.

FREE-STANDING SUPPORTS

SINGLE STAKE
Push in right to the bottom. Useful for single-stemmed dot plants and trees

BRUSHWOOD
Push twiggy branches into the compost when plant stems are about 6 in. high

CANE WIGWAM
Push in right to the bottom — tie tops securely. Variant — leave canes upright

CHICKEN-WIRE ROLL
Make a cylinder of chicken wire and push it into the compost. Secure with canes

CIRCULAR SUPPORT
A range is available 1-4 ft (30-120 cm) high. Push the legs firmly into the compost

WIRE HOOPS
Stout galvanised wire is bent into shape and pushed into the compost

SUPPORT FRAME
A range of wood and plastic shapes and sizes is available. Push into the compost

GROWING BAG SUPPORT
Several proprietary types are available — buy a stout one for robust plants

WALL SUPPORTS

WOOD TRELLIS
The most popular form of wall support — mesh size 4-8 in. (10-20 cm)

PLASTIC MESH
Inexpensive, but requires firm fixing. Not suitable for heavy climbers

WIRES
Plastic-coated straining wire is pulled taut between the wall fixings. Wires should be stretched about 1 ft apart

PROTECTING IN WINTER

Containers without plants do not pose a problem in winter, but there are two exceptions. Terracotta pots and troughs which are not rated as frost-proof should be protected — move them indoors or cover them to keep the surface dry. Jars can also be damaged in a severe winter if left filled with compost — frozen compost can result in the neck being broken around the constricted opening, so remove some of the compost before the big freeze-up.

Containers filled with plants during the winter months have become more popular in recent years. Trees, shrubs, bulbs and spring-flowering bedding plants have long been around, but the advent of Universal Pansies has resulted in winter floral displays in containers everywhere. In many cases both the container and the plants it contains can be expected to come through the winter without harm, but there are important exceptions.

Firstly, the plants. If they are not really frost-hardy then the containers should be moved into a conservatory or frost-free but well-lit room indoors — alternatively the plants should be lifted and potted up for overwintering indoors. If this is not possible then some form of frost protection must be applied to these specimens during their winter stay outdoors — see below. Even hardy plants may need some treatment — it is a good idea to tie string around the branches of column-like conifers

and the leaves of Cordyline so as to reduce their spread. Shake snow off the branches of trees and shrubs if it is weighing them down.

Next, the containers. The danger here centres around badly insulated pots — plastic, terracotta, fibreglass, thin wood, metal and earthenware. If the container is small there is a real danger in a severe winter that all the compost will be frozen solid and the plant roots may then die. Some form of protection is necessary — see below.

PLANT PROTECTION

STRAW
Wrap plastic netting around the plant and tie loosely. Push straw between branches and netting

SACKING
Drape sacking over a tender evergreen. Easy to do, but less effective than the straw technique

HORTICULTURAL FLEECE
Drape horticultural fleece over the plant and tie loosely. More effective than the sacking technique

CONTAINER PROTECTION

SOIL
Plunge the pot up to its rim in a sheltered spot. Easy and effective but waterlogging is a danger

BUBBLE PLASTIC
Wrap bubble plastic around the pot and tie with wire or string. Preferred technique for large pots

SACKING
Sacking around the pot will protect to some extent, but straw between sacking and pot helps greatly

CHAPTER 6
CONTAINER TROUBLES

Container growing involves two separate sorts of problems. The container itself (pot, trough, tub etc) may be unsatisfactory and/or the plants it holds may fail to grow properly or may not grow at all. As outlined below the various problems which beset containers can usually be tackled without much trouble, but plant problems are generally more complex and more troublesome.

The things you grow in pots, window boxes, hanging baskets etc are subject to the same basic troubles which can beset similar plants grown in a bed or border. They can be attacked by pests or by disease, especially as they are often planted closely together. Aphids suck their sap, mildews whiten their leaves and vine weevils may eat their roots. It is fortunate, however, that the most popular type of container plant (the bedding plant) is less prone to attack by the various insects and fungi which can be such a nuisance on vegetables, hardy perennials and fruit. In addition, plants in containers are to some degree isolated from others in the garden, so that some pests such as slugs are less likely to be a problem.

This does not mean that the cultivation of annuals and bulbs in containers is trouble-free. Things do go wrong, especially for the inexperienced, but this is much more likely to be due to a cultural or environmental fault than a specific pest or disease. Plants die, others stand still for weeks after planting and in some cases the floral display is disappointing. In the garden the cause of these troubles is often poor soil, inadequate drainage or too little sunlight, but using good quality compost in a portable container means that these adverse factors can be largely or totally avoided. But it is all too easy to forget that restricting the roots to live in a small amount of compost in a pot raises its own serious problems — the plant is reliant on you for regular feeding, regular watering and adequate protection of its roots against frost if it is to overwinter outdoors.

The golden rules are to try to prevent trouble before it starts and to deal with it promptly as soon as it is seen. Don't ignore these rules which are described on pages 118–119. In a large bed or border a few plants with dead stems or wilted flowers may be masked by surrounding foliage, but the relatively few plants in a window box or hanging basket are a centre of attention. Still, the small number of plants in a container compared with a bed or border has its advantages. It is relatively simple to keep an eye on the leaves and flowers, and both protective and remedial measures do not usually involve a lot of time and expense.

PROBLEMS WITH CONTAINERS

Make sure that the new container you have bought is satisfactory. Wooden ones should be watertight, terracotta ones should be resistant to frost if they are to be left outside all year round and all should have adequate drainage holes.

Containers do deteriorate with age and so regular maintenance is necessary. Cracked clay and terracotta pots are generally discarded, but with an expensive one you can remove a cracked section and glue it back with Superglue. Rust on metal containers should be dealt with promptly — treat with a tannin-based rust digester and then paint the surface. Softwood is always a problem — paint with a plant-safe preservative at regular intervals and replace any rotten sections which you find. Repairing chipped concrete or reconstituted stone is not easy — a mortar/PVA adhesive mix will be sound enough, but matching the colour is a problem. Finally, plastic and fibreglass. Plastic which has become brittle because of sunlight should be discarded, but kits are available for repairing damaged fibreglass.

PREVENT TROUBLE BEFORE IT STARTS

CHOOSE A SUITABLE CONTAINER

Buy as large and deep a container as you can afford and which will be in keeping with the situation, so as to reduce the risk of dry root problems. To reduce the risk still further choose a self-watering pot. For permanent planting you will need a container with good insulating properties (wood, reconstituted stone etc)

BUY GOOD QUALITY STOCK

Most plants are bought as seedlings, rooted cuttings or dormant bulbs rather than being raised at home by the gardener. Do buy good quality stock — reject soft bulbs, lanky or poorly coloured bedding plants, unhealthy shrubs and disease-ridden perennials. Avoid at all costs buying plants which are offered for sale well ahead of the recommended planting time

PLANT OUT AT THE RIGHT TIME AND IN THE PROPER WAY

Ensure that greenhouse-grown plants have been hardened off before they are put outdoors — failure to do so can lead to lack of growth. Equally important is the need to wait until the danger of frost has passed before planting out half hardy subjects. Place the empty container in position — if it has been used before make sure that the inside has been thoroughly cleaned. Follow the planting or potting rules on page 17 — this will prevent air pockets being left around the roots of the new plants

CHOOSE SUITABLE PLANT VARIETIES

Make sure each variety you plan to grow is suitable for your location. Use the A-Z guides and avoid types which are likely to be too tender for your part of the country. Never choose sun-lovers for growing under trees or in other shady areas

FEED AND WATER PROPERLY AND REGULARLY

These requirements are absolutely vital if you want healthy and vigorous plants. Do not apply daily dribbles in dry weather — water thoroughly until it starts to come out of the drainage holes. With standard composts you will have to start feeding after 6–8 weeks. Follow the instructions on the fertilizer pack — with most brands this will call for application at regular intervals. With slow-release fertilizer, however, a single treatment will last for months

CHOOSE A SUITABLE COMPOST

There is no such thing as a truly 'universal' compost. You will need an ericaceous one for lime-hating plants such as Azaleas and added grit for alpines. Buy a soil-based one for permanent planting and either a soilless or soil-based one for seasonal planting using bedding plants, bulbs etc. Always use a soilless compost where weight can be a problem

RAISE GOOD QUALITY SEEDLINGS OR CUTTINGS

Do the right thing at the right time. Read the propagation section in the appropriate book — The Bedding Plant Expert, The Garden Expert etc. Use clean trays and fresh shop-bought compost for raising seedlings indoors. Prick out before overcrowding occurs and remember to hold the seedlings by the leaves and not the stems. Check if the plant dislikes transplanting — if it does then prick out into peat pots or cellular trays rather than into ordinary seed trays

PROVIDE WINTER PROTECTION

Leaves and stems of hardy plants can suffer some damage from snow or frost in a severe winter, so some form of protection may be necessary. Even more serious is the danger of the compost freezing solid. If possible move the pot indoors if it is small, portable and poorly insulated. If a planted-up container has to stay outdoors over winter then some form of protection (page 116) should be provided

DEAL WITH TROUBLE WITHOUT DELAY

INSPECT PLANTS REGULARLY

Keep an eye on the plants growing in tubs, pots, hanging baskets etc. Drooping leaves are generally a sign that the soil around the roots is dry. Dead blooms on some bedding plants have to be removed to prolong the flowering period. This regular inspection is especially important with vegetables and fruit where pests and diseases can get quickly out of hand. If leaves, stems or fruit are damaged, distorted or discoloured check in The Vegetable Expert or The Fruit Expert to see if treatment is required

EXAMINE DEAD PLANTS

There will be times when a plant growing in a container will die for no apparent reason. Lift it out without delay and look at it closely before replacing with another plant. It may well have been killed by an environmental factor such as frost, overheating or drought (see pages 120–121) but it may also have died because of the roots being attacked by an underground pest such as vine weevil. If a pest or disease can be seen on the roots or in the compost around them then replanting in the same compost may well be a waste of time and money

REMOVE OCCASIONAL PROBLEMS BY HAND

Minor attacks by caterpillar or leaf miner can often be controlled by picking off the insects by hand. Trim away dead branches or leaves which are mouldy from plants which are basically healthy. Remove stems with all-green leaves growing on a variegated variety

KEEP A FEW SPARE PLANTS

It is a good idea after filling containers to keep some plants in a pot or tub in an out-of-the-way spot or in a spare patch of ground in the garden. In this way gaps can be filled if early losses occur

KEEP A FIRST AID KIT

Some people keep a stock of a few multipurpose pest killers for emergency use, but do not hoard a chemical armoury — it is better to buy a new small container when needed rather than keeping packs from one season to another

SPRAY PROMPTLY AND PROPERLY IF NECESSARY

Don't leap for a sprayer every time you see a stray insect or a few holes in a leaf, but there may be occasions when a serious pest or disease attack threatens the display or crop. A heavy infestation of caterpillars or greenfly calls for immediate action, and there are a few diseases which should be treated as soon as the first symptoms appear

Before you start	• Read the label carefully. Make sure that the product is recommended for the plant you wish to spray. If it is to be used on a fruit or vegetable check that the harvest interval is acceptable • Follow the instructions — do not make the mixture stronger than recommended
When and how to spray	The weather must be neither sunny nor windy During the flowering season spray in the evening, when bees will have stopped working Leaves should be dry Use a fine forceful spray. It is wise to keep all sprays off your skin. Wash off any splashes Do not spray open delicate blooms Spray thoroughly until the leaves are covered with liquid which is just beginning to run off
After you have finished	• Wash out equipment, and wash hands and face • Do not keep the spray solution to use next time • Store packs in a safe place. Do not keep unlabelled or illegible packs — throw in the dustbin after emptying liquid down an outside drain. Never store in a beer bottle or similar container

Cultural Problems

Many things can go wrong because container-grown plants have to rely on both you and the weather to provide their basic needs. Fortunately very few of these potential problems are likely to affect decorative seasonal planting using bedding plants and bulbs — the two commonest cultural faults here are underwatering and underfeeding. With permanent planting these common cultural faults are joined by the failure to protect the containers against freezing conditions in winter.

FEW OR NO FLOWERS

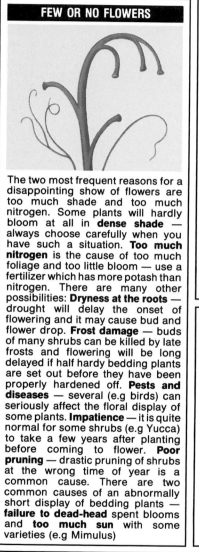

The two most frequent reasons for a disappointing show of flowers are too much shade and too much nitrogen. Some plants will hardly bloom at all in **dense shade** — always choose carefully when you have such a situation. **Too much nitrogen** is the cause of too much foliage and too little bloom — use a fertilizer which has more potash than nitrogen. There are many other possibilities: **Dryness at the roots** — drought will delay the onset of flowering and it may cause bud and flower drop. **Frost damage** — buds of many shrubs can be killed by late frosts and flowering will be long delayed if half hardy bedding plants are set out before they have been properly hardened off. **Pests and diseases** — several (e.g birds) can seriously affect the floral display of some plants. **Impatience** — it is quite normal for some shrubs (e.g Yucca) to take a few years after planting before coming to flower. **Poor pruning** — drastic pruning of shrubs at the wrong time of year is a common cause. There are two common causes of an abnormally short display of bedding plants — **failure to dead-head** spent blooms and **too much sun** with some varieties (e.g Mimulus)

DRY COMPOST

If you fail to water regularly and properly during the summer months the symptoms of drying out will appear. At first the leaves wilt and then the lower ones turn yellow and then fall. Eventually the plant dies. Water the compost and sprinkle the leaves at the first signs of wilting — leaving it any longer will lead to irreversible damage. Read the Watering section (pages 112–113)

WATERLOGGED COMPOST

Waterlogging causes leaves to turn limp and soft — if prolonged the stem bases and roots start to rot. There are several possible causes — compost made with heavy soil, insufficient or blocked drainage holes, or failure to follow the instructions when making slits in a growing bag

SPRING SCORCH

Bright sunny weather after a cold spell surprisingly leads to browning or death of evergreens instead of active growth. The cause is cold-induced drought — sunshine and drying winds stimulate water loss from the leaves, but the roots are not active and cannot replace the loss. Spray newly-planted evergreens with water in spring — provide protection from frosts and east winds

SUN-SCORCHED LEAVES

Brown patches sometimes occur on the foliage during a hot and dry spell in the summer. If these patches are dry and there is no sign of disease then the cause is probably sun scorch. Water droplets on the surface following watering act as small lenses — in summer always water in the morning or evening

SNOW-DAMAGED BRANCHES

The weight of snow in winter on the branches of an evergreen will usually do no damage, but a heavy snowfall can damage a branch of a large specimen tree. Gently shake the branches to remove most of the snow, but if a heavy fall is forecast tie the branches of a choice conifer together with twine

TWISTED LEAVES

The leaf stalks are twisted spirally and the leaves are narrow and twisted. The stems are distorted and reddish. The cause is a lawn weedkiller which has been allowed to drift on to the plants — never treat the lawn on a windy day, and never use a watering can for both weedkilling and watering plants

FROZEN ROOTS

In a severe winter the compost in a container may be frozen solid. The result is that the roots of trees, shrubs or perennials it contains are damaged and may be killed, which results in the death of the plant. The risk is greatest when the container is small and thin — protect such pots, troughs etc by moving them indoors or by covering them with suitable insulation (page 116)

OVERHEATED ROOTS

The result of roots being baked in a hot summer is similar to the effect of being frozen in a cold winter — the plant is killed. This is only likely to be a problem when a number of risk factors come together — a container which is small, shallow, dark-coloured, poorly insulated and exposed to the sun all day long. Make sure that at least some risk factors are removed

COLD-DAMAGED LEAVES

Frost will severely damage or kill half hardy plants — a fact known to any experienced gardener. Less well-known is the fact that a sudden cold but not frosty snap in spring can affect developing leaves by destroying chlorophyll. The affected leaf when it expands may be yellow edged or almost white. Pick off affected leaves — spray with a foliar feed

POT-BOUND ROOTS

A specimen tree or shrub in a container will become pot-bound in time. Look for the symptoms — slow growth even when fed regularly in summer, compost which dries out very quickly and roots growing through the drainage hole. Remove from the pot for the final check — a mass of matted roots with little compost visible. Pot on or repot — see page 17

STARVED PLANTS

It has been stressed in several parts of this book that feeding is required a few weeks after planting. You can either apply a standard fertilizer regularly or use a controlled-release feed which lasts for months. If you don't feed the plants then one or more deficiency symptoms will appear

Nitrogen shortage

Stunted growth
Small, pale leaves
Weak stems

Apply a balanced fertilizer

Potash shortage

Brown, brittle edges
Small flowers
Low disease resistance

Apply a balanced fertilizer

Iron shortage

Lime-haters affected
Large yellow areas
Young leaves worst

Use an ericaceous compost

Manganese shortage

Lime-haters affected
Yellow between veins
Oldest leaves worst

Use an ericaceous compost

OVERCROWDED PLANTS

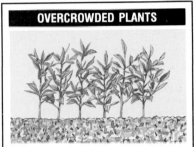

Bedding plants are placed more closely together in a container than in a bed or border, but planting too closely can result in tall and weak stems which are prone to disease. Delicate types such as Mimulus can be swamped by vigorous ones such as Nasturtium. Avoiding overcrowding is even more important with permanent planting

LANKY PLANTS

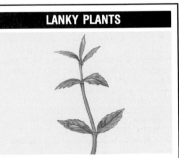

There are three possible causes for spindly, weak growth. The plant may be receiving too little light, so move to a sunnier spot. It may be starved, so apply a liquid balanced fertilizer. Finally, it may be too close to other plants, so thin out plants if practical. With bedding plants nip off growing points to induce bushy growth

SLOW-GROWING PLANTS

This is only a problem during the period of active growth between spring and autumn — growth slows down naturally in winter because the day-length is short and the temperature is too low for active growth. Shortage of nitrogen is a cause of slow growth in the active season, but feeding will not help if there is another cause. Overwatering can be the culprit, especially if the drainage is poor. A pot-bound plant will grow slowly (see above) and so will many sun-lovers if placed in a shady spot. An even more common cause is trying to grow a somewhat tender variety in a cold and windy location, or putting out bedding plants while the weather is still cold

Pests & Diseases

As the whole range of garden plants can be grown in containers it is not surprising that the list of potential enemies is enormous. Few, however, are a problem with the types of plants most commonly grown in pots and tubs — bedding plants, bulbs and conifers are more likely to be troubled by environmental faults. There are still a number of insects and fungi which can prove troublesome in some seasons — these are described and illustrated here.

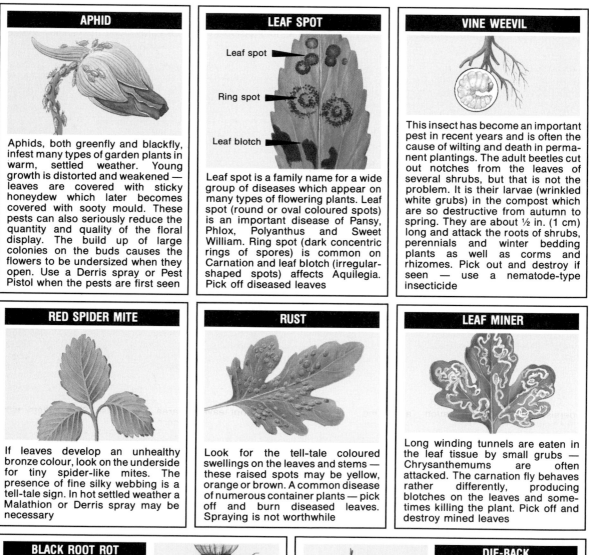

APHID

Aphids, both greenfly and blackfly, infest many types of garden plants in warm, settled weather. Young growth is distorted and weakened — leaves are covered with sticky honeydew which later becomes covered with sooty mould. These pests can also seriously reduce the quantity and quality of the floral display. The build up of large colonies on the buds causes the flowers to be undersized when they open. Use a Derris spray or Pest Pistol when the pests are first seen

LEAF SPOT

Leaf spot

Ring spot

Leaf blotch

Leaf spot is a family name for a wide group of diseases which appear on many types of flowering plants. Leaf spot (round or oval coloured spots) is an important disease of Pansy, Phlox, Polyanthus and Sweet William. Ring spot (dark concentric rings of spores) is common on Carnation and leaf blotch (irregular-shaped spots) affects Aquilegia. Pick off diseased leaves

VINE WEEVIL

This insect has become an important pest in recent years and is often the cause of wilting and death in permanent plantings. The adult beetles cut out notches from the leaves of several shrubs, but that is not the problem. It is their larvae (wrinkled white grubs) in the compost which are so destructive from autumn to spring. They are about ½ in. (1 cm) long and attack the roots of shrubs, perennials and winter bedding plants as well as corms and rhizomes. Pick out and destroy if seen — use a nematode-type insecticide

RED SPIDER MITE

If leaves develop an unhealthy bronze colour, look on the underside for tiny spider-like mites. The presence of fine silky webbing is a tell-tale sign. In hot settled weather a Malathion or Derris spray may be necessary

RUST

Look for the tell-tale coloured swellings on the leaves and stems — these raised spots may be yellow, orange or brown. A common disease of numerous container plants — pick off and burn diseased leaves. Spraying is not worthwhile

LEAF MINER

Long winding tunnels are eaten in the leaf tissue by small grubs — Chrysanthemums are often attacked. The carnation fly behaves rather differently, producing blotches on the leaves and some-times killing the plant. Pick off and destroy mined leaves

BLACK ROOT ROT

A common disease, affecting Antirrhinum, Begonia, Sweet Pea, Geranium etc. Above ground the leaves turn yellow and wilt. Below ground the roots are blackened. There is no cure, so avoid the causes — do not use dirty containers, do not make compost using unsterilized soil and do not replant the same type of plant in infected compost

DIE-BACK

A serious problem of a wide range of trees and shrubs grown in containers. It begins at the shoot tips and progresses slowly downwards. There are several possible causes, including diseases such as canker. If no disease is present, waterlogging is the likely cause. Cut out dead wood and paint the surface with a wound sealant

VIRUS

Viruses may be carried by insects, tools or fingers. There are many different symptoms — leaves may be yellow, covered with yellow spots or patches ('mosaic'), crinkled and distorted or white-veined. Stems may be covered with brown stripes ('streak') or stunted and distorted. There is no cure, but fortunately bedding plants are rarely bothered. Buy healthy stock — keep aphids under control

GREY MOULD (Botrytis)

Grey mould is a serious disease of annual plants in wet seasons. A fluffy mould appears on the leaves — with many plants (Petunia, Zinnia, Tomato) stems are also attacked. Blooms may also be affected — petals are spotted at first and then become rotten. Pick off mouldy leaves and flowers as soon as they are seen. Destroy badly diseased plants. Spray with a systemic fungicide

POWDERY MILDEW

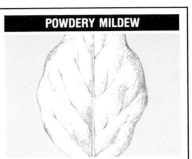

Like grey mould this can be a serious disease, but powdery mildew is encouraged by dry conditions in the compost rather than an over-wet environment. It is also encouraged by overcrowding. This disease attacks numerous bedding plants (Chrysanthemum, Aster, Verbena etc) and Roses. Spray with a systemic fungicide at the first sign of disease and repeat as instructed on the package

CATERPILLAR

Many different caterpillars attack container plants — look for rolled leaves and large irregular holes in the foliage. Some are uncommon but a few such as the angle shades moth can be serious pests. Pick off the caterpillars if practical — if damage is widespread spray with a persistent insecticide such as Fenitrothion

WOODLOUSE

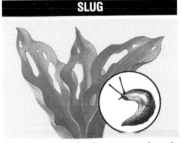

An abundant pest in shady gardens — during the day they hide under containers and at night enter through the drainage holes and into the compost. Roots may be attacked, but this insect is rarely a serious problem. No chemical treatment is necessary, but do not leave rubbish in the garden

SLUG

The leaves of plants growing in containers stood on the ground may be devoured by these serious pests, but other plant parts such as bulbs, tubers and rhizomes may be attacked. Slugs and snails generally hide under containers and garden rubbish during the day, so keep the area clean. Use Slug Pellets with care

BIRDS

Birds are extremely selective in their choice of plants to attack. Most flowers are ignored but some are not — Polyanthus, Crocus and Sweet Peas are examples. The flower buds of some shrubs may be stripped in winter or early spring, but it is fruit in containers which are most in danger. With ornamentals there is no simple answer — netting is unsightly and repellants are rarely effective. Surprisingly, flowers and flower buds in one garden may be ruined but similar plants next door may be spared. The bird problem is one you have to live with if you are growing ornamentals, but netting may be essential with some fruit types (e.g Plum, Cherry, Gooseberry) if you are to harvest any fruit at all

SCALE

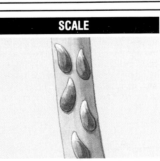

Several types of scale may be found on the branches of many trees, but their lifestyles are generally the same. The adults spend their lives in one place on the stem, protected by a hard shell. Their feeding on the sap causes a loss of vigour. Brush the affected area with methylated spirits or rub off with soapy water

CUCKOO SPIT

These frothy white masses are a common sight on many plants grown in containers — bedding plants are the ones which are mainly affected. Cuckoo spit is produced as a protective mechanism by colonies of froghoppers — tiny insects which suck the sap and distort young growth. It is rarely worth spraying — just hose off gently with water

CHAPTER 7

PLANT INDEX

Acknowledgements

The author wishes to acknowledge the painstaking work of Gill Jackson, Paul Norris, Linda Fensom and Angelina Gibbs. Grateful acknowledgement is also made for the help or photographs received from Heather Angel, Pat Brindley, D Askham/The Garden Picture Library, J Bouchier/The Garden Picture Library, L Brotchie/The Garden Picture Library, B Carter/The Garden Picture Library, D Clyne/The Garden Picture Library, J Glover/The Garden Picture Library, S Harte/The Garden Picture Library, N Holmes/The Garden Picture Library, M Howes/The Garden Picture Library, Lamontagne/The Garden Picture Library, J Legate/The Garden Picture Library, J Neubauer/The Garden Picture Library, C Nichols/The Garden Picture Library, H Rice/The Garden Picture Library, J S Sira/The Garden Picture Library, Tania Midgley, Harry Smith Horticultural Photographic Collection, Joan Hessayon, Carleton Photographic, Elizabeth Whiting & Associates, Di Lewis/Elizabeth Whiting & Associates, Marie O'Hara/Elizabeth Whiting & Associates, Dominic Whiting/Elizabeth Whiting & Associates, David Lloyd/Elizabeth Whiting & Associates, Jerry Harpur/Elizabeth Whiting & Associates, Jeremy Whitaker/Elizabeth Whiting & Associates, Apta Terracotta Pottery, Capital Garden Products Ltd, Haddonstone Ltd, C H Brannam Ltd/Hammond Visual Media Communications, Loral Products Ltd, Olive Tree Trading Company, Stewart Company and Sunware UK Ltd.

John Dye provided both artistry and design work.